I0796560

CLAY

Easy Air-Dry Clay Projects to Make at Home

SARAH REEVES

CONTENTS

INTRODUCTION

As an artist and designer, I love to craft and create for every occasion. Air-dry clay holds a very special place in my heart, and I've been drawn to it for its versatility and accessibility (no wheel or kiln is needed), but also for the therapeutic nature of working with clay.

I have been creating and sharing my air-dry clay projects for many years over on my Red Rocking Bird YouTube channel, where you can find lots of resources to explore.

In this book I'll share with you a wide collection of creative and easy-to-follow project ideas for the home, all made from air-dry clay and using minimal tools. I love designs that are both beautiful and practical. The projects will start off simple, and as we progress through the book I'll introduce new ideas and techniques, alongside little tips and tricks. You'll gain a multitude of new skills that will allow you to move forward and let your creativity flourish.

The projects in this book are here for inspiration, so you can follow them exactly as described or put your own spin on them. Don't worry if projects and ideas don't turn out as you expected – experimentation and enjoying the creative process are just as important as your finished piece. When things don't quite go to plan, this can be an opportunity to change or adapt to achieve a different end result. After all, clay is a forgiving medium – you can always start a new project or take a fresh slice of clay out of the pack. Try things out and develop new methods – we are all learning all of the time.

Clay is a great way to bring people together – it is a versatile craft medium for everyone, from young children to experienced artists – and in this book you will find many projects to enjoy with loved ones. All you need to do is buy a block of clay and get stuck in!

Sarah

@redrockingbird

1
2
3
4
5
6
7
8
9
10
11
12
13
14
15
16
17
DAS
THE BEST TO MODEL YOUR IDEAS

MATERIALS & TOOLS

A block of air-dry clay is all you really need to begin your journey into clay. I really believe our best tools are our hands, and many items from our day-to-day lives can also be used as tools. I like to see what I have around my home to craft with, and you will pick up lots of tips throughout this book to help you use what you have and be creative, especially when you start out. That being said, here is a list of the basic kit I would recommend:

AIR-DRY CLAY

This clay (7) is exactly what it says on the packet – air-dry – meaning that the clay hardens naturally when exposed to the air. Unlike ceramic earthenware clay, air-dry clay doesn't require a kiln to harden; you don't even need an oven (as you do with polymer clay, which is also popular among crafters). Homemade air-dry clay is another option, but it doesn't always work for all the techniques in this book, e.g. the score and slip method (see p.20). Personally, I find that the ingredients of homemade clay add up to about the same cost as purchasing a premade block of clay, so the ease of ready-to-use packs usually wins my vote!

When shopping for your clay, look out for the words 'air-dry' or 'air-hardening'. To confuse matters, air-dry clay can have 'modelling clay' written on the pack (this usually refers to malleable clay that doesn't harden), but this is followed by the words 'air-hardening', and that's what's important.

Air-dry clay typically comes in 1kg blocks (2.2lb), but of course you can also get smaller packs of 250g (8.8oz) or 500g (17.6oz), and much larger packs (5kg; 11lb). There are many brands available, such as DAS (13), Jovi and Scola. In this book I use my preferred air-dry clay, DAS white, which is a putty-like colour when wet, and gets gradually lighter as it dries to a pure white. You can also purchase air-dry clay in other colours – for example, terracotta (orange) or stone (grey) – if you prefer.

Air-dry clay 'light' or air-dry clay 'foam' are different again. These come in a huge range of colours but don't have the same texture as regular air-dry clay. They feel more plasticky, and, once dried, are very lightweight. I once added water to a fully dried piece, and it instantly turned to mush! These clays can be sealed to prevent this, and they do have their uses, but they are not the same as the 'regular', paper-based air-dry clay that I use in this book.

WORK SURFACE

The key thing is that this surface is smooth and non-porous. I use tiles left over from our bathroom renovation and I find these provide a good, non-stick surface. Alternatives are a smooth glass or plastic chopping board, or a wooden board. A piece of fabric on a work surface is also an option. A damp cloth can be used to clean up surfaces.

ROLLING TOOLS

A rolling pin (9) or any other smooth cylindrical object, such as an empty glass bottle, works well to roll clay flat. I've used the barrel of a marker pen to roll out my clay on occasion! In the first chapter of this book, we'll be rolling the clay a lot.

CUTTING TOOLS

A table knife (14) or a scalpel work well to cut the clay into the shapes you need for each project, as well as for cutting clay from your block. Alternatively, a flat ruler (15) can be used to cut straight edges into the clay – simply hold it along your cutting line and press down firmly into the clay. This results in a lovely straight edge, which is really useful in many projects.

To cut more detailed shapes into the clay, I sometimes use a sewing pin or needle (4). A plastic drinking straw (2) is very effective for cutting small holes into the clay – for example, to thread twine through once the clay is dry.

Cookie cutters (11) work well with air-dry clay and there are many amazing designs. I have a set of really useful circular cutters that range in size from 20 to 120mm (¾–4¾in) in diameter. The one I use most is 90mm, or 3½in. Don't worry if you don't have the exact size specified in this book; work with what you have or use a knife to cut around a cup/bowl.

SMOOTHING TOOLS

It is useful to have a small pot of water nearby when you're working with clay. You can lightly dip your fingers into the water and use them for smoothing the clay. For smoothing larger surfaces, use a damp sponge. Any fine sponge works here – I use a new kitchen sponge with the scourer cut off. Alternatively, a damp paintbrush can help you get into the finer details. Air-dry clay slip (5), which I will talk about in the 'Techniques' section (p.19), is also a great alternative to water for smoothing the clay.

SUPPORTS AND ARMATURES

When making 3D clay pieces, you can use ceramic and plastic bowls as supports to help shape and hold up your clay while it dries. Rolled-up tin foil (12), plastic balls (10) and other non-porous objects are also useful for this. These are taken away once the clay is dry.

Armatures are internal structures that support the clay, and these stay inside the clay permanently. I use tin foil, wire and sometimes pebbles and ping-pong balls, as the 'skeleton' inside the clay. I introduce the use of armatures towards the end of this book, in chapter 3 (see p.97).

SANDPAPER

Once the clay is fully dry it can be sanded to smooth out any imperfections. It is important that you do not breathe in the particles of air-dry clay, as this could be a health hazard. Work in a well-ventilated area, or sand outside if possible. I wear a half-face respirator mask that dust particles cannot penetrate. I cannot smell anything through this mask, so it would also be useful if you are thinking of trying out any resin crafts.

Fine-grit sandpaper of around 200 grit is what I use (3); the larger the number, the finer the paper. Avoid coarse sandpaper for finishing as it may leave scratch marks.

TEMPLATES

Templates can be used to help cut clay shapes accurately or to make many copies of the same shape. You can find the templates used for the projects in this book on pp.131–41. You will need tracing paper, a pencil, scissors and card to transfer these templates. You can, of course, create your own templates by drawing freehand designs or printing designs from the internet to cut out and use. I love using templates as they save time, allowing you to create the same project again and again with ease. It's a good idea to keep your templates all together in a file so you have them on hand when you want to use them.

PAINTBRUSHES

Expensive paintbrushes are not needed but a mixture of flat and round acrylic brushes in a range of sizes (16) is useful if you want to decorate your air-dry clay pieces. Brushes can be used for painting as well as applying varnishes and sealants. Ideally, keep a couple of brushes just for varnishing so that they do not have any traces of paint left in them, as these could seep out and distort your project. Always wash your brushes well after each use. Acrylic paint (1) dries quickly, so it's best not to leave brushes hanging around with acrylic paint on them. A quick tip: I often use the wrong end of a paintbrush as a tool for marking the clay – another way to really make use of what's on hand.

PAINTS

I mostly use acrylic paint with air-dry clay. The brand of paint is up to you, but I would avoid the very cheap paints as you really do get what you pay for. Occasionally I also use watercolour paints (see, for example, my Hanging Pot on pp.76–9). I recommend testing out techniques and experimenting to find a style you love.

I tend to buy paints in the primary colours of red, blue and yellow, along with black and white, and mix the desired colours from these (17). Take a look at colour theory and a colour wheel if you are not familiar with mixing colours – you can save money by not buying millions of tubes of paint, and it's a great part of the creative process.

VARNISHES AND SEALANTS

It is important to finish your pieces with sealant or varnish (8); the latter is really just a sealant with the aesthetic advantage of giving a particular finish. Otherwise they are likely to get damaged. There are a wide range of sealants and varnishes available and choosing the right one can be daunting. When I get asked what to seal the clay with, I say it's a good idea to start with what you have at home from previous craft or DIY projects, as most craft varnishes can be used with air-dry clay. You can test out sealants and varnishes on small scraps of air-dry clay, let them dry and see what you think of the finish.

If you want to buy something specific, I would recommend a water-based acrylic craft varnish to begin with. This is easy to apply with a brush, low-odour, fast-drying and washes out of brushes in water. The gloss variety can also give a lovely sheen. Many brands are available.

Then there are solvent-based varnishes (with various drying times). These can have a strong odour, and brushes need cleaning with a solvent like white spirit. Check the packaging carefully before making your choice: solvent-based varnishes are often marked as flammable. I also use oil-based polyurethane varnish, which is very durable, but this can sometimes yellow, takes a long time to dry and can have a strong odour. Brushes also need washing in white spirit after use. Water-based polyurethane varnishes are also available.

I finish and seal some of my air-dry clay projects with UV resin, making the items super shiny and even more durable, but this is not recommended for complete beginners, and it's not the best for the planet. Spray varnishes and lacquers in a can are handy, too.

Varnishes tend to come in gloss, satin and matt finishes, so plenty of choice. Drying times vary, so it's best to consult the packaging and test it out first; the same goes for how many coats of varnish to apply.

MATERIALS TO CREATE PATTERNS

Creating texture and pattern on the clay is worth exploring. I use objects such as straws, toothpicks, sand, pebbles, forks, buttons, dried seed heads and foliage – pressing them into the clay to make patterns. Plenty of ideas are included in this book; in the Textured Coasters project (pp.41–3) I show you how you can make your own tools to create beautiful patterns in the clay.

EXTRA MATERIALS

Here are a few other items that are useful to have on hand:

- Matchsticks
- Chopsticks
- Lollipop sticks
- Toothpicks
- Ruler
- Pencil
- Scissors
- Hot-glue gun and glue sticks
- Craft wire
- Twine/string for hanging items
- Jam jars/yoghurt pots

KEY TECHNIQUES

There are some core techniques and useful tips that I will share with you here, so that you can refer to them when necessary.

CONDITIONING YOUR CLAY

Air-dry clay fresh from the pack can be rolled and sculpted straight away, but if we need to form, for example, a ball of clay, then we can condition and knead the clay first. This technique is also really important when we use leftover clay from a project – we can bring the clay back together in a neat ball, so we don't waste any.

The flat palm of your hand is good for kneading large pieces of clay back together; knock the clay into shape by tapping the clay into this part of your hand, then knead and roll into a ball. I find that all of this starts to loosen the fibres of the clay. There will be cracks in the surface where the clay has come together; smooth these over with your thumb until they all disappear. For me this is an important preparation, making for a smoother project in which less cracks will form. If you start off with a crumbly, cracked piece of clay, the final piece is more likely to be crumbly and cracked: 'start smooth to end smooth' is my motto!

ROLLING YOUR CLAY

Many projects begin with a slab – an evenly rolled out piece of clay. Place a block or ball of clay on your smooth work surface and take a rolling pin (or similar) and roll the clay using gentle, even pressure. Roll several times and then pick up the clay and rotate it, and then repeat until the clay is at the desired thickness. When teaching others in person, I am always repeating, 'roll and turn, roll and turn', just like my Mum always did when I was a child, making cookies or pastry. This ensures an even roll and stops the clay being forced into the surface and sticking. For extra help in achieving an even thickness on your clay slab, you can place stacked lollipop sticks or chopsticks on either side of the clay, or just blocks of wood, and roll the rolling pin over these. As you practise, however, you'll get a feel for the clay and it will all come naturally.

Once it is rolled out, smooth over the clay with your fingers or something like a business/credit card. The clay slab is then ready to cut to shape.

SMOOTHING YOUR CLAY

Water can be used to smooth the clay, but use as little water as possible, because adding too much may encourage the clay to form cracks. Air-dry clay shrinks a little while drying as the moisture within it evaporates. Air-dry clay slip (see right) is a great alternative to water. I often use my fingers to smooth the clay, but a damp brush or a damp fine sponge can also be useful.

MAKING SLIP

Air-dry clay slip is the 'glue' that we can use to help attach two pieces of air-dry clay together. It is also great for helping to fill cracks if they occur. Slip is simply a mixture of air-dry clay and water. Take a small jar or tub with a lid. Pinch tiny bits of air-dry clay with your fingers until flat and put them in the jar with roughly the same quantity (in volume) of water, I tend to boil the kettle and use this water, as it speeds up the process and 'cleans' the water first. Stir loosely together, pop the lid on and leave the mix to do its magic for a few hours or overnight. Then, stir until smooth.

You will get an idea of how thick you can make the slip as you gain experience: I like mine the consistency of thick yoghurt. If you feel it is too thin in consistency, leave the lid off for a day and it will thicken up. If you feel it is too thick, add a bit more water. I make small quantities at a time because it can go mouldy when left too long. I also make slip from dried air-dry clay, and from the air-dry clay dust left over from sanding – these are great ways of reducing waste.

JOINING CLAY

When joining two slabs of clay (see the Incense Stick Holder and Tealight Holder projects in this book, pp.65–71), the edges can be securely joined using the score and slip technique. Score (crosshatch) the two joining surfaces with a sharp implement like a pin or toothpick, scuffing the surfaces that will join. Paste some air-dry clay slip onto one of the scored surfaces and then press the two scored surfaces firmly together. Clay can then be scraped from one side of the join to the other to bind the gap. A thin coil of clay (see right) can be added all along the join and smoothed down in the same way to give extra strength to the joint.

SLAB BUILDING TECHNIQUE

A slab of clay is clay rolled out to a certain thickness, which is then cut to size and formed into a design. When joining two slabs together it is best to use the score and slip technique (see 'Joining Clay', left).

MAKING COILS

A coil of clay is basically a sausage of clay. I often use coils as little 'walls', and also for extra strength when joining clay after using the score and slip method (see left).

Roll a smoothed piece of clay between your hands or against the table to elongate the shape. To make a much longer coil, place both hands on top of the clay and roll the clay forwards and backwards, spreading your fingers out and pushing your hands

outwards simultaneously. Keep going, slowly and evenly, until you reach the correct coil diameter. Create these when you need them rather than ahead of time, to prevent them from drying out before use.

PINCH POT TECHNIQUE

The pinch pot technique is a very popular method of making pots and vases with traditional clay, and the same can be done with air-dry clay by creating a paddle with your fingers. I explain this method in the Hanging Plant Pot project (pp.76–9).

CREATING TEXTURES

A great alternative to smooth clay is to add texture. Also, some projects can be fairly tricky to get completely smooth, e.g. if they are large or have an unusual shape – adding texture means you don't have to sand the clay! Texture can be added with a chunky paintbrush, a toothbrush, scrunched up tin foil or other tools; pressing these with various degrees of pressure into the surface of the clay will create different effects. Items with patterns on can also be used to imprint the clay. The Textured Coasters project (pp.41–3) is a great starting point for this technique. There is also the possibility of adding to the surface of the clay, e.g. with sand, as I do on the Textured Clock in chapter 2 (pp.73–5).

SANDING YOUR CLAY

Once dry, sanding gives your piece a smooth finish, making it ready to be varnished or painted. To get into tight spaces, a small piece of sandpaper can be glued to the end of a knife or pencil. To achieve a flat surface, you can use a small block of wood wrapped in a sheet of sandpaper.

PAINTING YOUR CLAY

Once the clay is fully dry it can be painted. Acrylic paint covers evenly and creates a rich colour. Often two coats of acrylic paint are needed; let the paint dry fully between layers (acrylic paint does dry pretty quickly, which is another advantage). I often give the piece a full base coat of colour first, before adding more colour and details. Adding a few drops of water to the paint allows the paint to brush on more smoothly, and into textures, but more coats of paint may be needed. Be as bold as you wish, or choose tones to match your decor.

Dry brushing is when you remove most of the paint from the brush, onto a rag or piece of paper, until the brush is fairly 'dry'. Brush this lightly over the piece to bring out texture, add depth, give a weathered look and highlight areas.

Once painted, a very important step is to seal the air-dry clay (see right). If you want any parts of your clay to be a crisp white, then I recommend painting the clay white before varnishing. Coating bare air-dry clay in varnish can result in an uneven finish and an off-white colour once fully dried. But experiment and find your preferences, as different projects require different results.

SEALING YOUR CLAY

Once air-dry clay is dry it is still porous and will absorb any moisture, therefore it may reactivate or become 'mushy' if not sealed. So, please make sure you include this important step in all your projects to preserve your hard work. Water-based varnishes are typically touch dry within two hours but must be left for at least twenty-four hours to cure completely. Apply the varnish with an acrylic brush and do not overwork, otherwise you may get brushstrokes or dull the varnish.

Once finished, wipe the brush on an old cloth, and clean following the pack instructions. Use gloss, satin or matt depending on the desired result.

FREQUENTLY ASKED QUESTIONS

When getting started with air-dry clay, you will likely have a lot of questions about how to use this new material. Below I've provided answers to the most common questions, and you can always ask me more over on my Red Rocking Bird YouTube channel, in the comments sections of the videos.

HEALTH & SAFETY

Air-dry clay is not food safe.
Do not make plates and cups etc. from air-dry clay for use with food. Ceramic clay that can be fired in a kiln is recommended for this.

While it is possible to waterproof your air-dry clay creations with polyurethane varnish or resin, this is difficult for beginners, and I would recommend using mugs for decorative purposes only, and placing smaller waterproof vessels inside your projects when needed.

Adult supervision is required while children use air-dry clay.

HOW MUCH CLAY DO I NEED?

I recommend purchasing clay in 1-kg (2.2-lb) blocks. When a project requires 250g (8.8oz) of clay, portion off roughly one quarter of the block (or use weighing scales if you prefer). Measurements are just a guide and there is normally some clay left over after each project. Change up the quantities and dimensions when you feel confident, to give each project some variation in size.

HOW THICK SHOULD MY CLAY BE?

For the projects in this book, which are all home decor items, I recommend rolling the clay to at least 8–10mm (approx. ⅜in) in thickness, to make them strong and robust.

When making 3D items, although we want them strong and robust, that does not mean we want a giant ball of clay. Ideally, the whole piece would have a fairly uniform thickness so that it can dry evenly, with as little cracking as possible. You can use an armature (p.12) to achieve this. I try to have the clay no thicker than 15mm (½in) in any part, so that it has a chance to dry, but items like the vases are hollow.

Other artists may create differently but what I share with you in this book has worked well for me over the years. At every stage, experiment and see what works for you. In some of my projects on YouTube I do roll the clay thinner – for small clay pins, etc. – but here in this book, where we are making larger items for the home, I roll no thinner than 8–10mm (⅜in), with the exception of the heart on the Little House Photo Holder (pp.36–9).

Work in your preferred method to produce the desired results, using this book as a guide.

HOW DO I STOP MY CLAY FROM CRACKING?

As air-dry clay dries it shrinks a little, and as it shrinks there is chance for it to crack, especially around any joints or at transitions between thicker and thinner sections, because the clay may have dried unevenly. If a crack of 1mm (1⁄16in) or more appears while drying then I tend to smooth on some water or air-dry clay slip (see p.19) and then take a small amount of fresh air-dry clay and press this into the crack, smoothing out until it is no longer visible. For hairline cracks the slip alone is a sufficient filler.

Really don't worry if you feel your clay piece that you have worked hard on didn't quite go as you wished. It is air-dry clay, it is very forgiving and yes, I have faith that it can be fixed. It is best to start with simple projects then build up to projects that are more complex so that you start to understand how the clay behaves and dries.

HOW DURABLE IS AIR-DRY CLAY?

I love air-dry clay and encourage you to create with it, but many people worry about it breaking. As with any ceramic item, there is a chance it might break if not looked after or if an accident occurs. I feel air-dry clay is far more durable than people think. To ensure your pieces are as strong and long-lasting as possible, my advice is to ensure your joins are secure using the score and slip technique described on p.20. As a beginner, avoid really thin sections of clay – don't, ideally, go thinner than 8mm (⅜in) for these projects. Designing strong, sturdy structures can help with durability.

Sealing the clay with certain top-coats can also really give extra strength and help protect your pieces. I have dropped air-dry clay from a height many times as a demonstration – it seems daft, I know, but thankfully most people are happily surprised by the outcome!

HOW LONG SHOULD I LEAVE MY CLAY TO DRY?

Many instructions for clay say to leave your air-dry clay to dry for 24 hours. I have always left my air-dry clay to dry for much longer than that. If you allow your clay to dry more slowly in a cooler environment, I believe fewer cracks will form, and over the years I have not really had trouble with air-dry clay cracking. (Though really don't worry if cracks appear, as they can often be fixed – see opposite.) With the white air-dry clay that I use, I can really see it change from a light grey to a pure white as it dries; it really is gorgeous and so satisfying once it has dried.

If you can, keep turning the piece over to allow even drying. I often find my clay is fully dry after about four days in a cool room with relatively low humidity, but different temperatures and humidities affect the drying of the clay. It's always better to leave it for longer, as it is important not to seal in any moisture – otherwise your work could go mouldy. So, personally, I always plan to paint/seal my clay a week after creating. The answer is slow, long drying – good things come to those who wait!

WHAT DO I DO WHEN I WANT TO TAKE A BREAK?

Sometimes we want to take a break while creating, and that is perfectly fine. Take a lightweight cloth, soak it in water and wring the excess water out, then place this cloth over the clay and place a plastic bag over the cloth and clay to try and keep the air out. If you are going to leave your piece for longer than a few hours or a day, then keep wetting the cloth to make sure it stays moist

Different climates will influence how quickly the clay may carry on drying. If the clay has dried out more than you had hoped by the time you come back, then take a look at the next question. There are ways around everything, so keep going and have faith in your creative ability.

MY CLAY HAS DRIED BUT I WANT TO CONTINUE.

No problem. Wet, with a little water, the area of air-dry clay that you would like to add to, then continue sculpting with fresh clay on top of this. This is very helpful when working on much larger pieces, or if you prefer to work for shorter lengths of time. You can complete one section, let it dry, and then move onto the next, blending the fresh air-dry clay onto the damp, dried air-dry clay. For example, on the Little Bird Cottonbud

Caddy project later in the book (pp.115–17), you could complete the bird body and head, let them dry and then wet the joining edge and move on to the tail (making sure you add any texture to the part that will dry).

I HAVE A NEW VARNISH/PAINT AND I AM NOT SURE IF IT IS OK TO USE.

If you feel unsure about anything at all then I always recommend making a test piece. Take a section of clay similar to that you are making with, let it dry and then test your new products on this. Leave to dry and see what you think. It is always best to do this rather than risking your hard work.

Sometimes projects don't quite go to plan, but don't worry – try and think of a creative solution to get around this, but please do remember, also, just to have fun.

CAN I SEAL WITH PVA GLUE?

I don't, personally, but we all work a little differently and find our own way. You can try things out and do a test piece if you are unsure (see previous question).

SHOULD I USE GESSO TO PRIME THE CLAY?

I don't use gesso, but other artists do; this would be used as a base coat or primer on the bare air-dry clay before painting.

I personally find it more crucial to fully seal the clay with a proper sealant at the very end of the project. If your acrylic paint has a tendency to peel, you could introduce this extra step to help rectify the problem, but I have never had a problem with using acrylic paint as the primer. Personal preference is key here.

HOW DO I STAY TIDY? AND HOW DO I CLEAN UP?

Air-dry clay can leave a residue on your hands and work surface. Soaking your hands in warm soapy water works well to wash away this dried clay residue. When I do workshops with clay, I fill a bucket with warm soapy water and put a flannel at the bottom and this works well if you want to wash hands regularly, dipping hands in and rubbing them on the cloth from time to time. The damp cloth can also be used to clean clay residue from surfaces. Tools can be washed in warm soapy water.

I recommend wearing an apron and cleaning your hands regularly while working so the dried clay on your hands doesn't affect the surface of your clay. You will know what I mean once you have witnessed 'clay-ey' hands! Remove rings and bracelets and push up your sleeves before you begin.

HOW DO I STORE MY CLAY?

Left-over air-dry clay should be wrapped up and sealed when not in use to keep the air out – you can tape the pack back up, wrap it in a plastic bag and place in a Tupperware tub until you next need it. Air-dry clay keeps for a good length of time, but this book will hopefully inspire you to keep your clay creations flowing.

CHAPTER 1

GETTING STARTED

This first set of projects has been designed to help you really get acquainted with the feel and behaviour of air-dry clay. This chapter concentrates on the slab technique – rolling your clay to a specific thickness and cutting out your shape. Countless possible projects open up once you have become proficient at this. Don't worry if the projects don't turn out quite as you first expected – practise, experiment and see what works for you. The journey can be just as enjoyable as the destination, and I have faith in you! If all else fails, roll up your clay, give it a good knead and start again. I wrote this book to inspire you to be creative, go wild and explore the possibilities, so let's begin.

FLOWER 'FROGS'

Flower 'frogs' are the perfect beginner project. Don't worry, there are no real frogs here. These are used to help keep your flowers in place when flower arranging. They are decorative and practical – a winning combination.

WHAT YOU NEED

250g (8.8oz) air-dry clay
Jam jar or similar vessel
Rolling pin or similar
Knife
Drinking straw
Water
Sandpaper
Paintbrush
Sealant

Optional

Cookie cutter
Thin card
Pencil
Scissors
Sponge
Acrylic paint

1. Roll the air-dry clay to 8mm (⅜in) in thickness, remembering to roll and turn, roll and turn, to give a gorgeous, smooth, flat slab of clay (see p.18).

2. We now need to cut our first shape out of the air-dry clay – a round piece of clay larger than your jam jar. For this you can use either a larger jar, a cookie cutter or a template (see template on p.132, if required). If using a cutter, choose one that is 25mm (1in) larger than the diameter of your glass jar or vessel and press firmly into the clay to cut your shape. Remove excess clay from edges by lifting it up and away. If using a template, place it on the rolled-out clay and cut around the edge with a knife.

   To make the design with the scalloped edges, as shown here, cut out a circle of thin card 25mm (1in) larger than the diameter of the jar, fold the circle in half three times, and then cut a curve at the outside edge. Cut the clay using this paper template and a knife to cut around the edges.

3. To make the holes for the flowers to go through, take a straw, hold it upright and press down through the clay. Start with a hole in the centre and then, either randomly or symmetrically, cut more small holes into the clay. Each time, remove the tiny piece of clay from the tip of the straw by squeezing it out. Use various sizes of straws if you can, or pen lids of different sizes will also work.

4. Once you are happy with the design, use your fingers, sponge or a paintbrush to smooth out any imperfections in the clay; a small amount of water can help with this.

5. Turn your jar or vessel upside down, gently lift the clay and place onto the jar base. Very gently press on the sides of the clay so that a small curve forms (so that the clay domes upwards).

6. Leave the clay to dry on the base of the jar. Don't worry, it won't stick! Once dry, you can lightly sand the 'frog' with sandpaper.

7. I have chosen to leave my flower frogs white to really make the flowers pop against them, but you could paint them any colour or pattern. If you would like them to be a crisp white colour then paint with white acrylic paint.

8. Seal (see p.22 for guidance on this step). I used a paintbrush to apply two coats of a water-based acrylic varnish that will resist water. These flower frogs won't be submerged in water and shouldn't be!

9. Add some water to the jar, place your new flower frog on top (dome upwards) and then arrange the flower stems through the holes.

TIP

If using a card template, place it on top of the clay and roll over with a rolling pin. This leaves an indent which is then easy to follow and cut out with your knife. The card template can be kept to reuse at a later date.

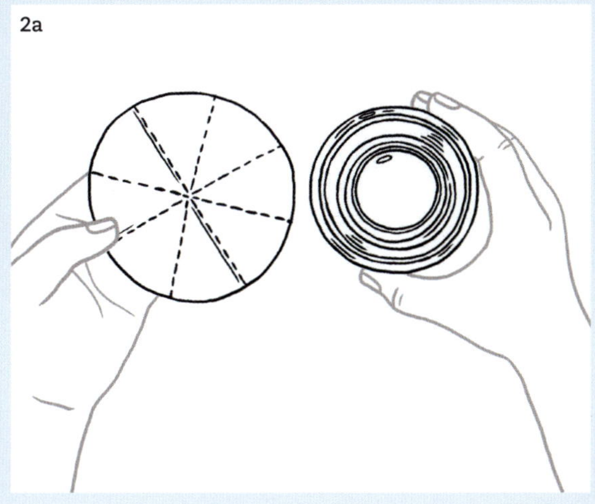
2a

2b

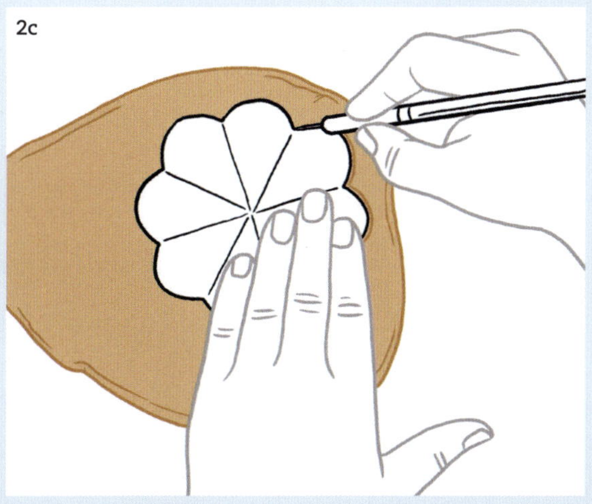
2c

3

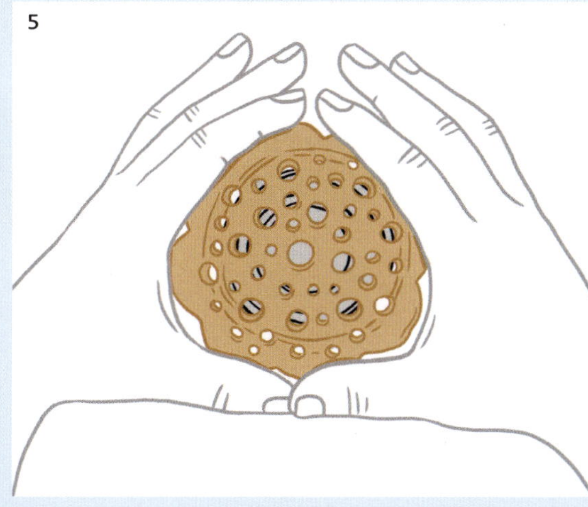
5

LITTLE HOUSE PHOTO HOLDER

These photo holders are easy to create and make wonderful gifts for loved ones. You can use the same basic method with different shapes and designs – why not try a heart, or a toadstool? Once dry and decorated, these can be used for displaying photos or postcards, or holding notes.

WHAT YOU NEED

250g (8.8oz) air-dry clay
Rolling pin or similar
Knife
Metal ruler
Water
Matchsticks
Chopsticks
Toothpick or similar
Galvanized/craft wire
Wire cutters
Sandpaper
Acrylic paint
Paintbrush
Sealant

Optional
Sponge

1. Start by rolling the clay to about 25mm (1in) in thickness – thicker than usual, to allow the little houses to stand up alone, and to allow for a slit where the photo/note will sit.

2. I usually cut a house shape like this by eye, but there are templates for you to trace in the back of the book (p.133). My little house is 30mm (1⅛in) wide and 45mm (1¾in) tall. My favoured way to cut straight edges into clay this thick is using a metal ruler. Hold the ruler perpendicular to the clay and press down firmly, slicing the clay straight. Then, at an angle, I cut away the corners for the roof.

3. Smooth the clay with fingers or a damp sponge.

4. Make indents in the front to depict windows and a door. Matchsticks and chopsticks are useful for this.

5. Stand the house upright and, using a ruler or piece of card, press into the top of the roof until halfway down into the clay. This is where the photograph will sit.

6. Roll a very small piece of clay, 6mm (¼in) in thickness, and cut a small heart shape with a scalpel or similar. Add a small hole with a toothpick, smooth and set aside to dry.

7. Cut a piece of galvanized craft wire 60mm (2⅜in) long. Bend the wire 10mm (⅜in) from the end, and hook this end into the 'roof' of the house, being careful not to let it disturb the slit or protrude out of the side of the clay. Smooth any gaps.

8. Set aside to dry, ensuring the slit that you made in step 5 remains clear.

9. Once fully dry, sand the clay pieces as required. To sand the inside of the slit, double over the sandpaper, insert into the gap and pull it backwards and forwards, ensuring the gap is large enough for a photograph.

10. Paint and seal all the clay pieces. I used acrylic paints and a water-based acrylic craft varnish.

11. Once everything is fully dry, thread the heart onto the end of the wire and loop the wire around to secure the heart in place. Take your photo and insert into the gap. I think a nice touch is to make more plain houses, without the photos, to display around it.

DECORATION SUGGESTION

To keep these simple, I painted the heart red and the door and roof a pale blueish grey. The heart is tiny, so to paint this I held it between my fingers, painted one side, let it dry a little, and then turned it around to paint the other side. Repeat if fuller coverage is needed.

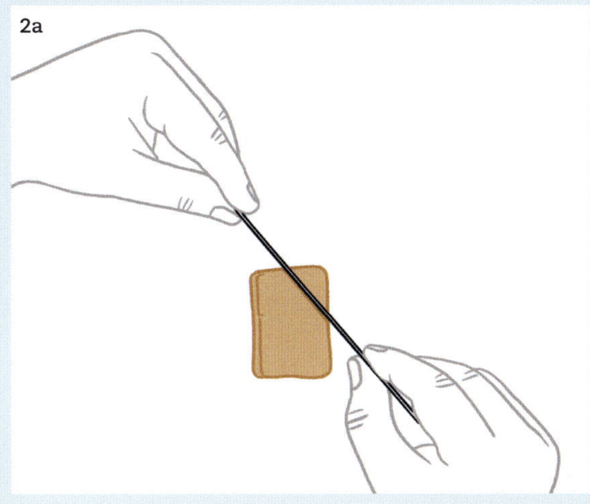
2a

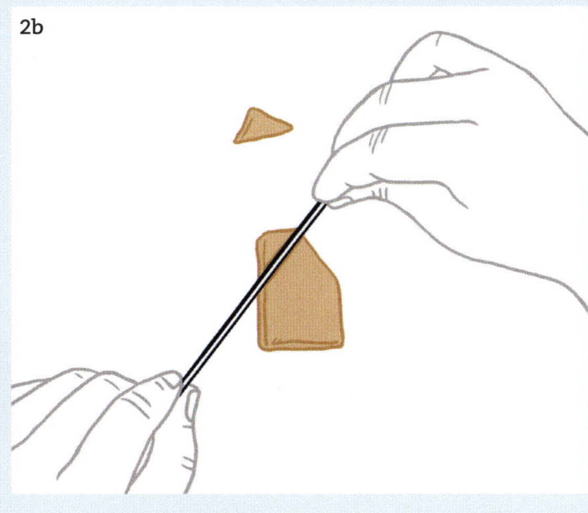
2b

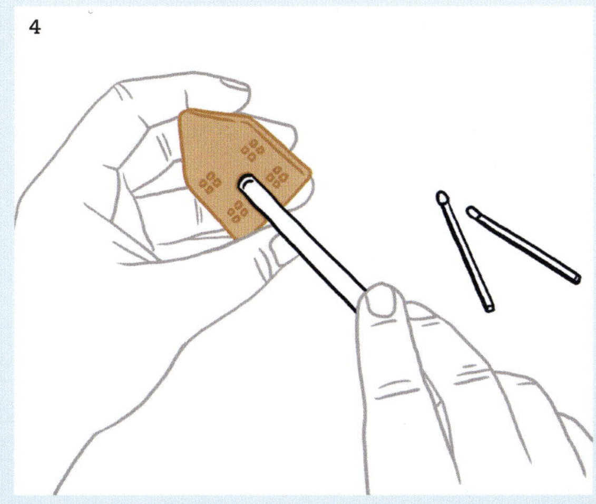
4

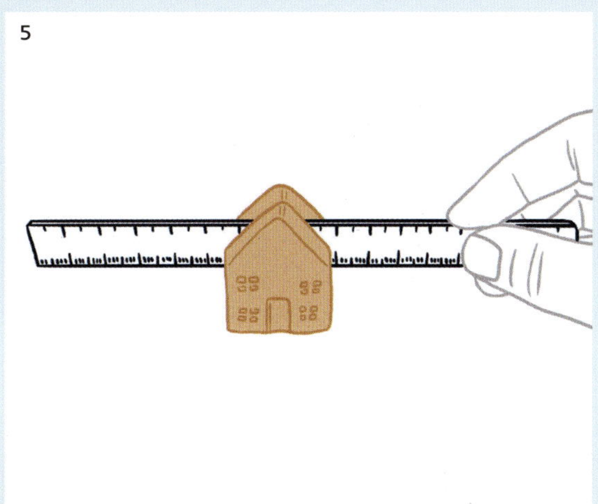
5

6

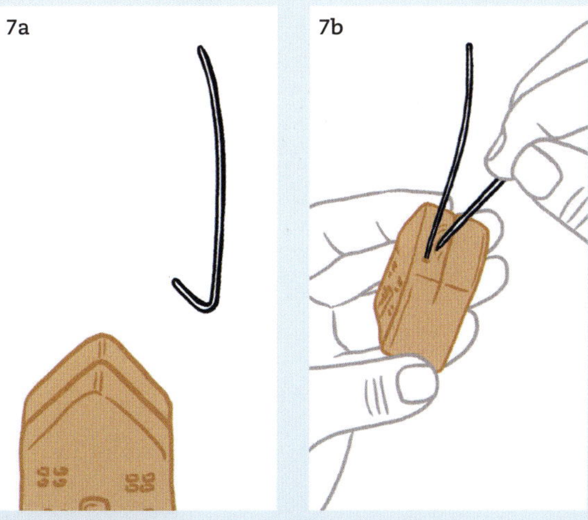
7a
7b

TEXTURED COASTERS

These pretty coasters are so practical. Imprinting in clay truly makes me happy, and you can see here how stunning the results can be, and without the use of fancy equipment. Let yourself loose and experiment with many possibilities with this one.

The imprinting tool is made from air-dry clay, too, and you will need to make this tool ahead of time, so bear this in mind when starting the project, as the tool will need to dry fully before creating the coasters. You can also use shop-bought stamps to imprint the clay if you wish.

WHAT YOU NEED

500g (17.6oz) air-dry clay
Rolling pin or similar
Round cookie cutters, 30mm (1⅛in) and 90mm (3½in), or larger
Needle or similar
Paintbrush
Sealant
Lollipop sticks
Acrylic paint
Sandpaper

Creating the tool:

1. Take a small ball of clay and roll to about 25mm (1in) in thickness. Cut a 30mm (1⅛in) circle, and then cut down to the board twice more, as shown in the illustration overleaf, so you end up with a fan shape.

2. Use the side of a needle to indent a pattern into the clay, as shown overleaf. Set aside to dry.

3. Once dry, apply a thin coat of craft varnish or sealant to your tool/s, preserving them, and leave to dry.

Coaster:

4. We want the coasters to be as even as possible. To help with this make two stacks of lollipop sticks, each about 8mm (⅜in) in height (tape together if necessary). Place these either side of a ball of clay and roll out the clay to create a clay slab.

5. Take your new tool and press into the clay by about 1–2mm (1⁄16in); lift and repeat to build up a lovely pattern. I made my first imprint in the centre and then worked outwards to build up the design. For contrast, I have only imprinted half of the surface of the clay. Once you are happy with the design, very lightly roll over the clay just once to ensure you have a fairly 'flat' surface but keeping all the detail.

6. Use the larger circular cutter to cut your coaster shape, ensuring that the pattern within the cutter is symmetrical.

7. Repeat this process for as many coasters as you wish to make, then leave them to dry fully. I leave mine on a smooth, non-porous tile – once fully dry they slide straight off.

8. Once dry, sand the edges if required, then paint the coasters in your favourite colour and seal. I used acrylic paint, then two coats of a gloss acrylic varnish. These coasters can then be wiped clean with a damp cloth, but I would avoid excessive heat.

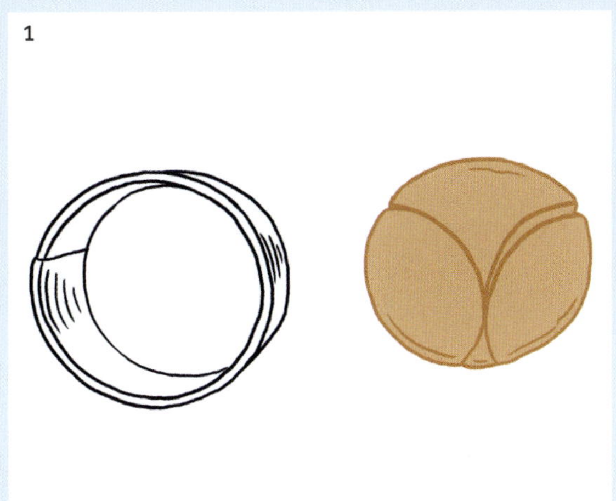
1

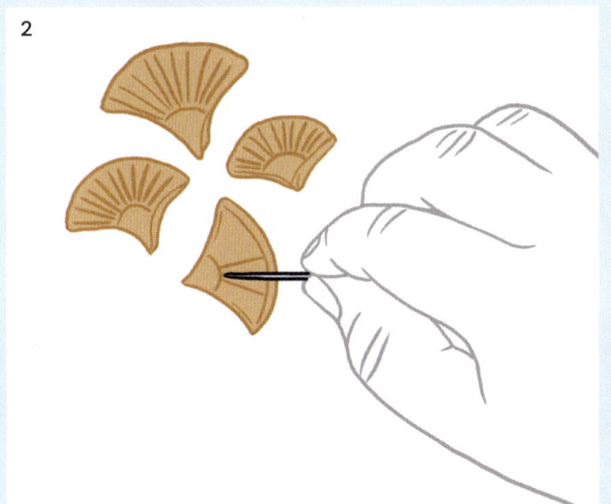
2

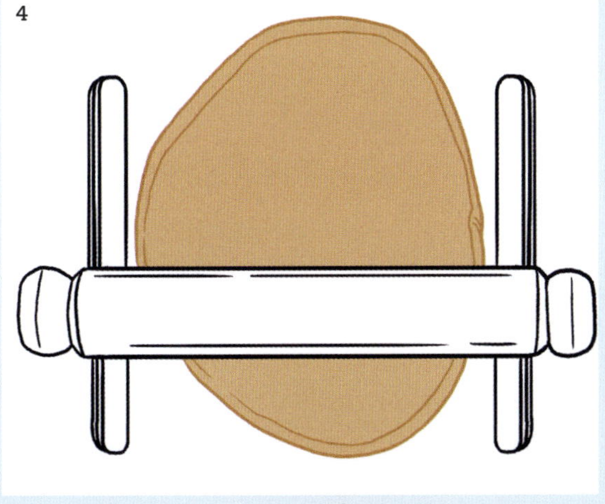
4

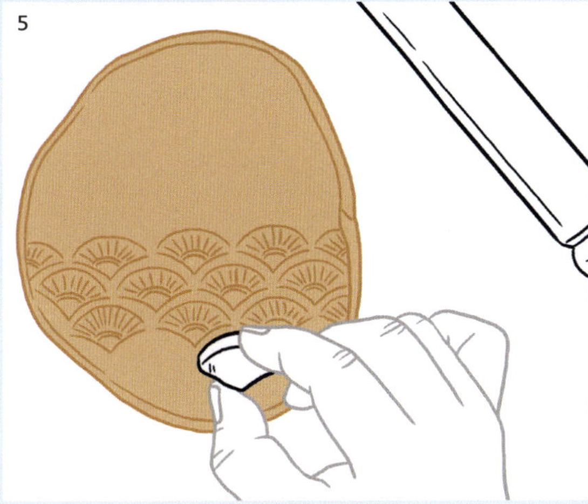
5

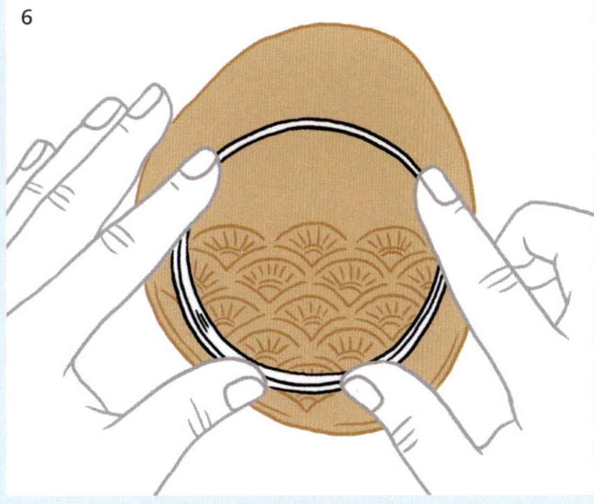
6

BOTANICAL RING HOLDER

A gorgeous addition to your bedside table or dresser, this ring holder is quick and easy to create. Using the basic technique of creating the grooves, you could then cut this into any shape of your choice. Have fun and be creative with imprinting the clay, too.

WHAT YOU NEED

250g (8.8oz) air-dry clay
Rolling pin or similar
2 chopsticks or similar
Knife/ruler
Pretty foliage
Paintbrush
Sealant

Optional

Cookie cutter
Acrylic paint

1. Form the air-dry clay into a smooth ball and roll to a thickness of 15mm (½in).

2. Place the chopsticks on top of the clay. I used the square ends, which were 6mm (¼in) wide, and placed them 9mm (⅜in) apart. Press the chopsticks down firmly into the clay with your hands or roll over with the rolling pin, until they are fully imprinted into the clay.

3. Imagine the shape you are going to cut out later – a triangle, in my case – and then place the foliage in the space next to the chopsticks. (Conifer foliage works well, or leaves with prominent veins/texture.) Roll over with the rolling pin, making sure the foliage stays in the same place. There is a template at the back of the book (p.134) if you would like a guide.

TIP

If your rings are on the larger side then make the grooves a bit deeper and wider. You can test them for size before the piece dries.

4. Gently lift away the foliage and chopsticks.

5. Take a knife or ruler (or cookie cutter, if you have one) and cut the indented clay into a triangle (or a different shape of your choice.

6. Smooth any edges as necessary and leave to dry fully.

7. Once dry, paint the ring holder with acrylic paint. I used an off white, being careful not to flood too much paint into the delicate foliage pattern, so as not to lose detail. Dry and seal. I used a matt varnish to finish.

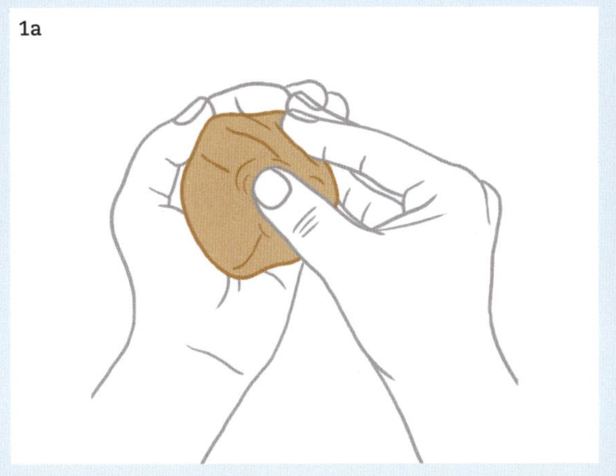
1a

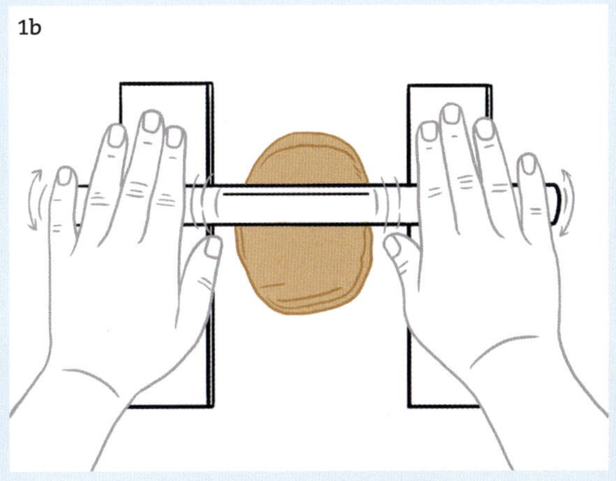
1b

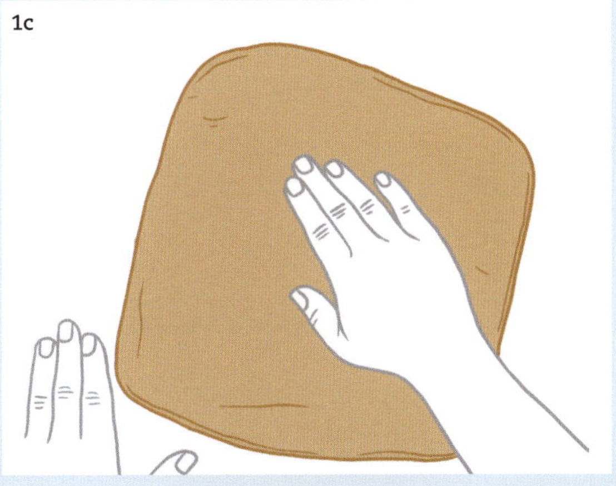
1c

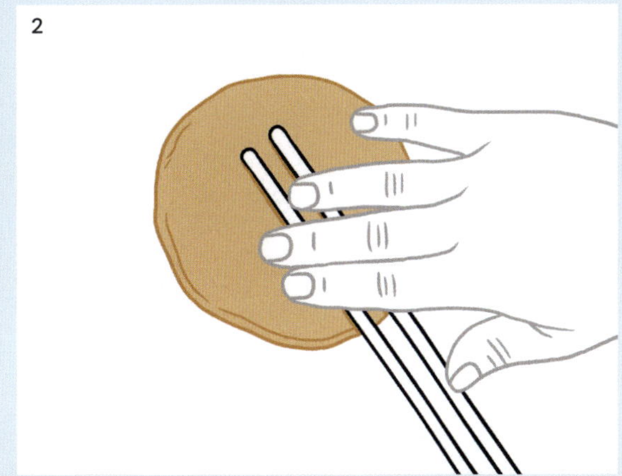
2

3

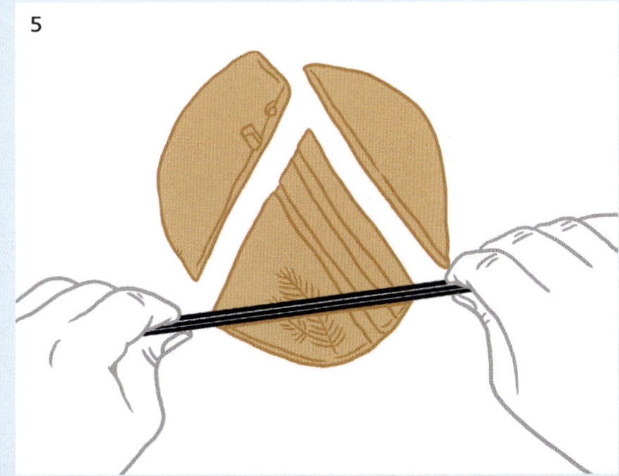
5

MOON PHASES BUNTING

Over the years I have made many strings of air-dry clay bunting, so here is an easy method to inspire you to create something beautiful for your next celebration. These moon phases are a lovely project for all year round. This bunting could also be adapted for festivals or a birthday with some painted-on lettering.

WHAT YOU NEED

1kg (2.2lb) air-dry clay
Rolling pin
Cling film
Round cookie cutter, 90mm (3½in) in diameter
Drinking straw
Sandpaper
Acrylic paint, white and a contrasting shade
Paintbrushes
Pencil
Sealant
1.5m (approx. 5ft) twine/string

Optional

Gold pen/gold leaf

1. Our aim here is to create seven equal discs of clay that are thick enough and strong enough to string together as bunting. Roll half of the clay out to about 8mm (⅜in) in thickness (rolling half at a time makes it easier to handle).

2. Take a piece of cling film a little larger than your rolled clay and lay this on top of the clay. Using a cookie cutter, cut out as many discs as you can from this first slab of clay by pressing the cutter against the cling film. The cling film should help to form a domed disc of clay.

3. Lift the cling film and then roll the remaining clay together and repeat steps 1 and 2 until you have seven consistently shaped clay discs.

4. To make the holes for hanging the bunting I used a straw to cut two holes, 40mm (1½in) apart, in each disc. Again, try to keep consistent; you could make a small paper template with two hole-punched holes and use this as a guide.

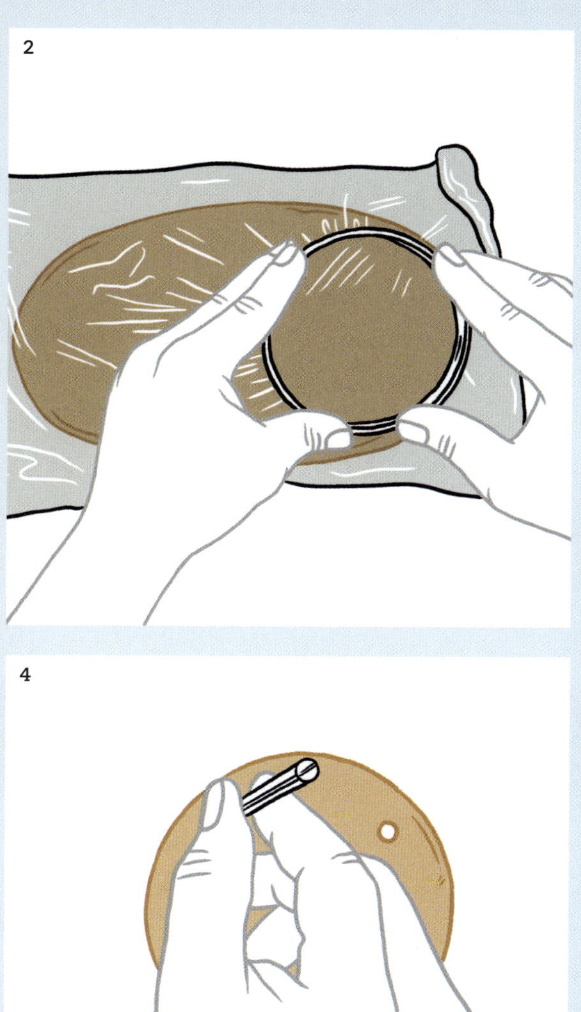
2
4

5. Smooth out any imperfections with your fingers or a brush, using a small amount of water if needed, then set aside to dry.

6. Once fully dry, sand with sandpaper if required and give the backs of the discs a coat of white acrylic paint, then leave to dry. Once dry, flip the discs over and paint the front. You may need to apply two coats of paint.

7. Take a pencil and draw lines for the moon phases onto the clay discs, using the edge of a cookie cutter or a cup/glass as a guide.

8. Paint in the detail with a darker acrylic paint colour, then leave to dry.

9. Mix a bit of water with some lighter-coloured acrylic paint and flick this onto the discs by tapping your paintbrush with another paintbrush, allowing speckles to fall onto the discs. This can be quite messy, so protect your surrounding area and clothes. Leave to dry.

10. To add some shine, I sometimes use gold leaf or gold pen. For this bunting I applied dots of gold pen randomly all over the discs. Take your time and enjoy the process.

TIP

If the discs start to curl as they dry, then I turn them over and gently press them back down. A smooth tile acting as a bit of weight can also be placed on top for part of the drying time. Don't be afraid to reshape the clay while it's drying.

11. Seal the clay. Spray varnish can be used for speed when varnishing many pieces like this, on a sheet of newspaper outdoors, letting one side dry fully and then turning over to spray the other side.

12. Thread the discs onto the twine, spacing them evenly. Tie a knot on each end, then hang and admire!

DECORATION SUGGESTION

To personalize these for a special occasion, trace some lettering onto the discs and paint in festive colours. Add splashes of paint in contrasting colours and metallic paint, pen or leaf for extra detail as you wish.

PRETTY MIRROR

This mirror will add a touch of contemporary chic to your home decor. For an alternative decoration style, you could simplify the curve and attach flowers or other shapes to the air-dry clay. Let this idea be a starting point for creating something that fits with your interior style.

WHAT YOU NEED

500g (17.6oz) air-dry clay
200mm (8in) round mirror
Rolling pin or similar
Table knife/ruler
Pencil/pen
Paper measuring at least 235 x 190mm (9¼ x 7½in)
Sponge
Sandpaper
Acrylic paint
Paintbrushes
Sealant
Super glue

TIP

Be gentle with this piece. In time it may need re-glueing if the mirror loosens itself from the clay. If you are giving this as a gift, then a really strong superglue is most definitely advised!

1. Begin by forming the clay into a coil approximately 300mm (12in) long, then roll lengthways to form a 10mm- (⅜-in) thick slab and cut a rectangle from this measuring 500 x 50mm (19⅝ x 2in). I used a metal ruler to cut this out.

2. Trace the template from the back of this book (p.135).

3. Lift the long slab of clay and tilt 90 degrees. Mimicking the bend of the template, begin to manipulate the clay into this shape. Be gentle and take your time. The clay will begin to crease and may seem a little bumpy, but persevere to get the desired shape. Place a book or a ruler along the straight edge – this is where the clay will rest on a surface when complete.

4. Smooth out the bumps and wrinkles with a damp sponge.

5. Leave to dry, turning over completely as needed, making sure it retains the overall shape and the flat base.

6. Once dry, sand, paint and varnish the clay wave. I used a matt varnish. See the decoration suggestion below for ideas.

7. Stand the clay upright, aligning the mirror behind it, as you can see on p.55. Mark on the clay in pencil where the mirror touches the clay. Take the mirror away and then apply superglue to the marked areas. Bring the mirror back up to the clay and hold in place with a few books in front and behind while the glue dries.

8. For extra stability, take a small, ping-pong ball-sized piece of air-dry clay and form this into a thick coil to sit behind the mirror. Allow it to dry and then paint, varnish and glue as above.

DECORATION SUGGESTION

I gave the clay two coats of a light-grey acrylic paint. Once this had dried, I added some shapes in a lighter colour with a flat brush. This would look gorgeous in vibrant colours to give any living space an extra lift.

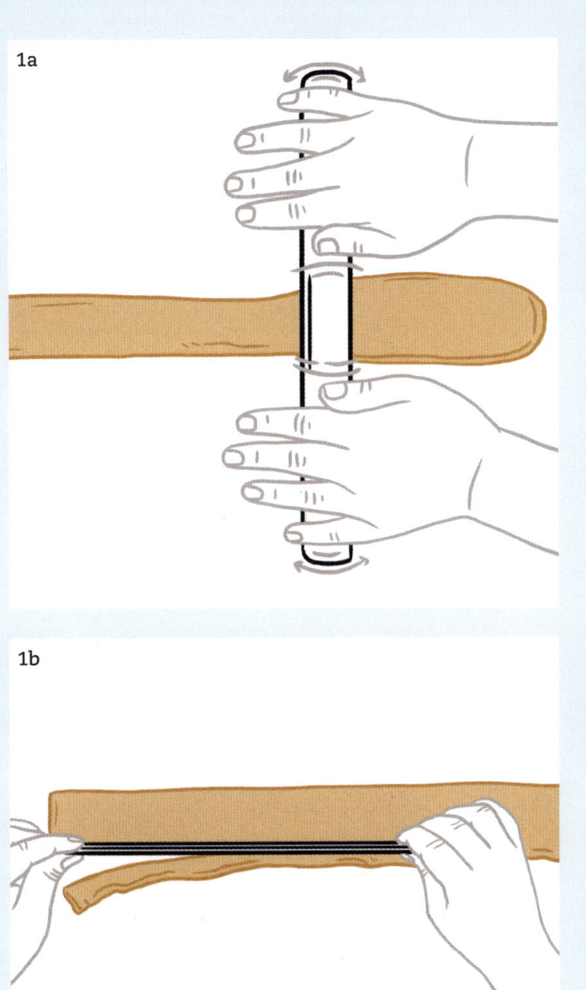
1a
1b

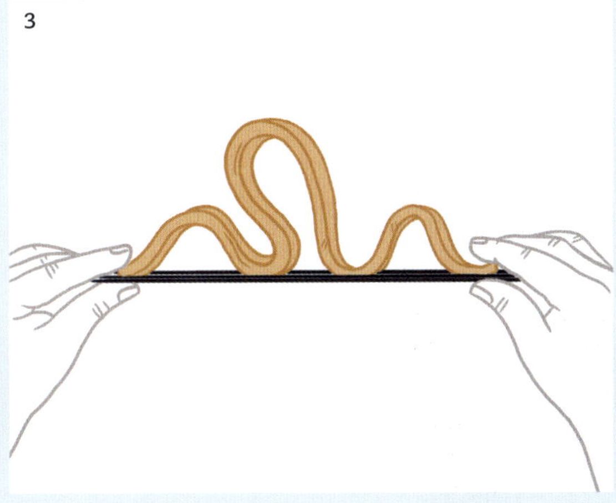
3

FLUTED DISH

Air-dry clay is wonderful for making beautiful pieces of home decor. In this project we create something a little bit bigger – a real statement piece for the home. But don't feel daunted – sometimes it is even easier to make items that are larger and less fiddly.

Although air-dry clay items cannot be used for serving food, there are many ways in which to use a beautiful dish like this in the home: for holding keys by the front door, on a bedside table or as a statement piece for the living room.

WHAT YOU NEED

1kg (2.2lb) air-dry clay
Long rolling pin or similar
Dinner plate or bowl
Parchment paper/cloth
Knife/scalpel
6 ping-pong balls/marbles or similar
Sandpaper
Acrylic paint
Paintbrushes
Sealant

1. Make sure you have a large surface to work on, and use the longest rolling pin you can find. I often use an old curtain pole sawn down to 300mm (12in).

2. Roll the clay to 10mm (⅜in) in thickness, using guides at the sides if that helps you achieve an evenly rolled slab of clay (see pp.18, 43). The roll-and-turn method is important here. Smooth the clay surface with your fingers, then turn over and smooth the other side, this makes sanding easier later on.

3. Lift the clay onto a large piece of parchment paper – it is helpful for moving the clay and making sure it does not stick to the work surface, though be warned that paper like this can also cause creases in the clay. Embrace the texture or be prepared to smooth or sand them out later. A piece of cloth could be used instead.

4. Take a plate or bowl just a bit smaller than your rolled clay. Mine was 270mm (10⅝in) in diameter. Place this upside down on the clay and make an indent. Lift off.

5. With your knife, cut this circle into the clay, following the indent and making sure you have a surface such as a chopping board underneath. Lift away the excess clay, knead it back together and wrap up and store until your next project.

6. Smooth out the edges of your large circle of air-dry clay if required.

7. Take the ping-pong balls and gently place them, one by one, underneath the edge of the clay. Space all six balls evenly (use as many as you wish, depending on the size of the clay).

8. Leave to dry. After 24 hours or less the clay will start to firm up. At this point I turn the dish over, smooth any creases out of the base and then leave to dry this way up (just make sure it can hold its shape before you do this). After some more hours drying, turn again if needed and dry fully.

9. Sand with sandpaper (or leave rustic).

10. I painted this one with two coats of acrylic paint (see my decoration suggestion, right). Remember to dry well in-between turning and coats of paint.

11. Seal. I used a gloss, solvent-based varnish.

DECORATION SUGGESTION

After painting the two sides of the dish in contrasting colours and leaving to dry, I drew a freehand floral pattern on the clay using a pencil. I then used a fine paintbrush and acrylic paint (matching that used on the underside of the dish) to add the pattern. (Alternatively, you can leave as a single colour, or add any other pattern you feel confident creating.) If you make a mistake with the pattern, just take a damp cloth and wipe off the fresh paint straight away; it should wipe away easily due to the acrylic base coat.

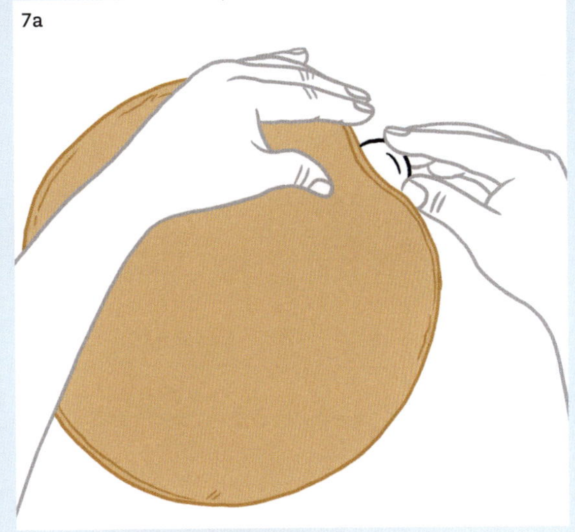
7a

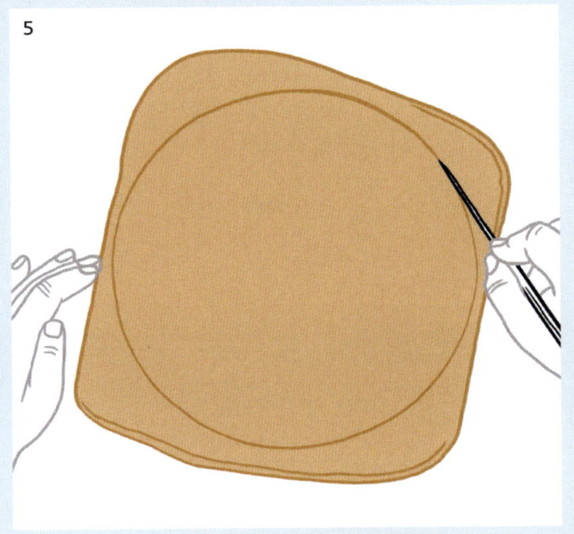
5

7b

5011386081557 DomRep

CHAPTER 2

A FEW MORE TECHNIQUES

In this chapter I introduce you to the score and slip method, which allows us to join two pieces of air-dry clay together. It is best if you avoid rolling your clay too thin, so that the pieces are more robust and easier to hold in place, especially as you start out. In traditional pottery, the pinch pot method is used for making pots and vases, and in this chapter, we make a lovely decorative plant pot using this technique (pp.76–79) Have fun creating these projects and embrace the new techniques. Practise as much as you can and try combining methods to create something new. Be bold and feel inspired!

INCENSE STICK HOLDER

Incense stick holders typically have a little dish that catches the fallen ash from the burning incense sticks. Any shape of dish can be created, so this is a great opportunity to really get creative, but I will show you just how simple it can be. This piece is based on a ginkgo leaf, and could also make a lovely trinket dish – just leave out the teardrop shape (step 4).

WHAT YOU NEED

400g (14oz) air-dry clay
Paper and pencil
Scissors
Rolling pin or similar
Sharp craft knife
Toothpick
Sandpaper
Paint
Paintbrushes
Sealant
Incense sticks

Optional

Damp sponge
Gold pens

1. Trace the template of the ginkgo leaf from the back of the book (p.136), cut it out and use it to cut the shape from a slab of clay 8mm (⅜in) in thickness (tips for rolling clay can be found on p.18 and in chapter 1).

2. Smooth the cut edges with your fingers or a damp sponge. I like to flatten the edges slightly and round them off.

3. Using a toothpick, make indents into the edges of the leaf, like little ripples, and then smooth these slightly with your fingers.

TIP

Tip out any ash after every burning and, if necessary, wipe clean with a damp cloth. Never leave burning incense sticks unattended and keep away from children and pets.

DECORATION SUGGESTION

I painted the whole piece in white acrylic paint and left it to dry. I then mixed a muted green tone of acrylic paint with a little water, and brushed this all over the piece. Using a cloth, I then wiped away some of the paint, leaving the darker paint in the grooves. Once dry, I used a gold pen (the kind that you need to shake to get going) and added some highlights over the green, in lines following the grooves. I sealed the project with a gloss acrylic varnish.

4. Make approximately 8g (¼oz) of clay into a round ball and then pinch into a teardrop shape. Flatten and score the underside of the teardrop; score the area of the leaf corresponding to the teardrop area on the template, also. Add some air-dry clay slip (p.19) and, with a bit of pressure, press these two surfaces together. Blend the teardrop shape down into the clay leaf. Smooth.

5. Taking your pencil or the end of a paintbrush, draw lines as veins, adding a little pressure to indent the clay. I add many lines, starting from the teardrop and running out to the edges of the leaf.

6. Take an incense stick and insert it into the middle of the teardrop of clay, as you would with the finished incense burner, to make a hole. Wiggle it slightly to make a bigger gap (this allows for just a little shrinkage in the clay when drying). Remove. Add some dot indents with the pencil all over the teardrop for texture.

7. To make this into a little 'dish' that has an organic form, I like to prop the edges up with various items, such as paintbrushes, pens, sponges or scrunched up paper. To add more shape, I put an inward bend on the stem.

8. Leave the holder to dry. When it has dried well enough to hold its shape, turn it over to continue drying, using a dry sponge underneath the piece if it needs some support.

9. Sand, paint and seal. See left for a decoration suggestion.

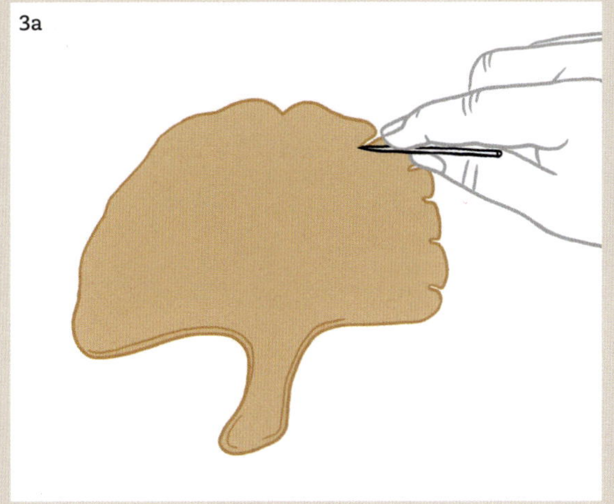
3a

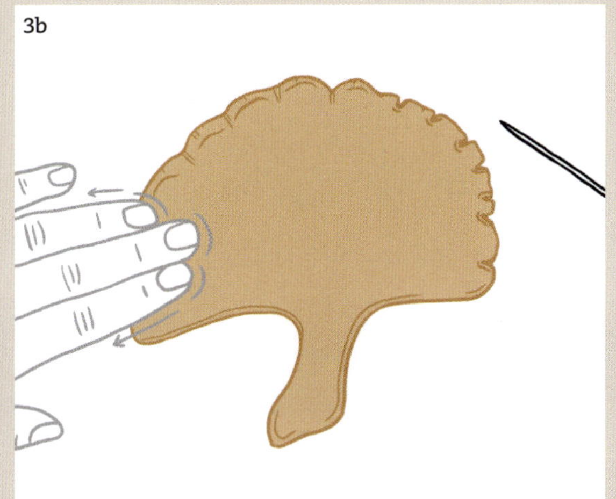
3b

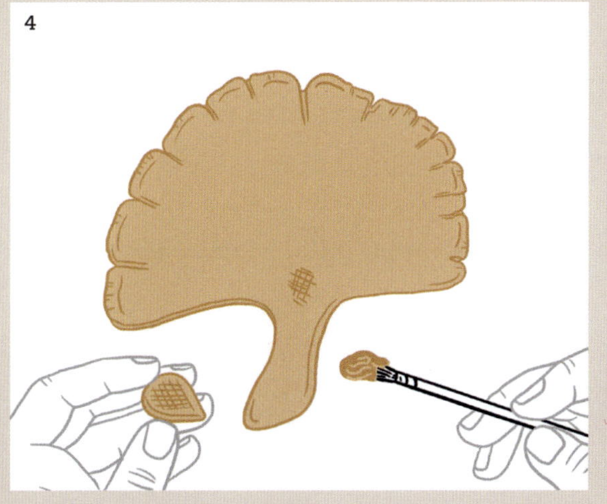
4

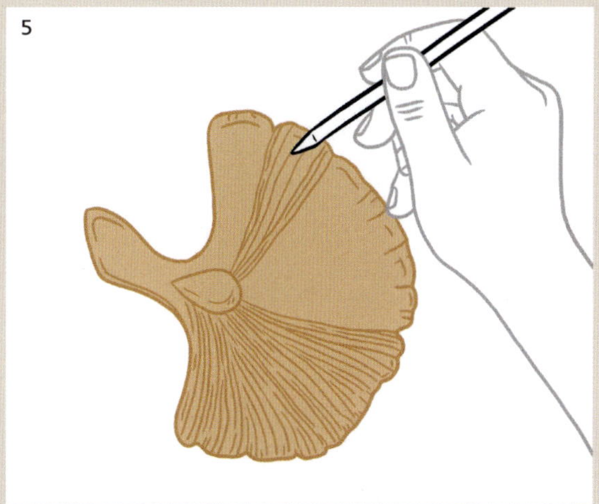
5

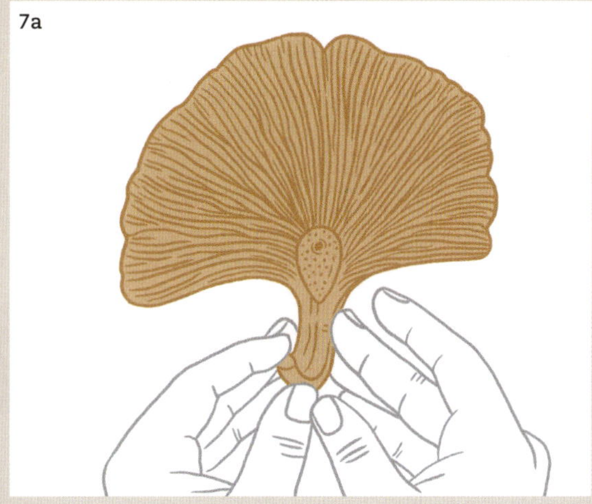
7a

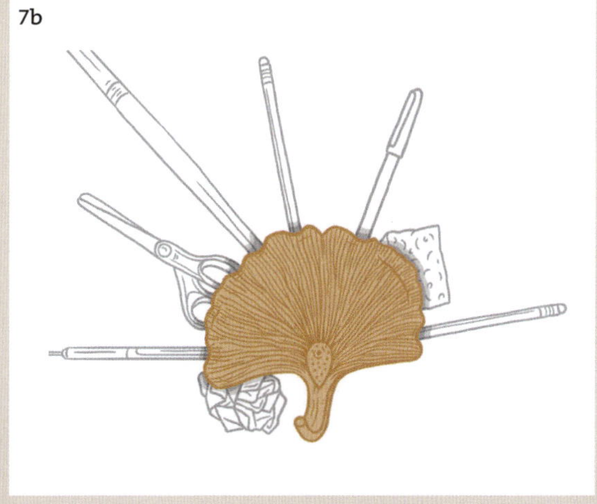
7b

TEALIGHT HOLDER

Everyone loves a candle (well, I do), and these little tealight holders will brighten up any table. Once you have mastered this project you could adapt it to different sizes and styles. The colours you paint your holders can give them a completely different feel, so don't be afraid to try out something new.

WHAT YOU NEED

250g (8.8oz) air-dry clay
Rolling pin or similar
Plastic ball, approx. 80mm (3⅛in) in diameter
Round cookie cutters, 30mm (1⅛in) and 90mm (3½in) in diameter
Scalpel
Sandpaper
Acrylic paint
Paintbrushes
Sealant

1. Using half of the clay, roll a slab 8mm (⅜in) in thickness and cut a 90mm (3½in) disc.

2. Smooth both sides of the clay disc and then lift it onto the plastic ball, gently teasing the clay to the shape of the ball with your hands. I like to smooth the 'outer' edge to a curve, leaving the inside edge, flush to the ball, as a sharp line, as this gives us a crisp edge to paint up to later.

3. Rest the ball on a small round cookie cutter or similar, so it can't roll, allowing the ball and clay to be put down.

4. Knead the remaining clay together. Roll to 30mm (1⅛in) in thickness and cut a 30mm disc. This is going to be the base of the candle holder, so you can adjust the height by altering the thickness of this clay if you wish.

5. Score one of the flat sides of this thick disc of clay. Also score the centre of the clay on the ball, as shown overleaf. Add some air-dry clay slip (p.19). Bring the two scored surfaces together, trying to get them as neatly matched as possible, and apply pressure to help secure.

6. Roll a thin coil of clay, as long as the circumference of the candle holder base, and put this around the join, blending the surfaces together using your fingers or a knife (p.20).

7. Take a scalpel and cut away some of the centre of the base. This gives the base a good shape and enables the clay to dry evenly. Use the end of a paintbrush or similar to smooth the hole.

8. Leave to dry for a few hours, with the ball still in place, until the base and outsides have started to firm up.

9. Twist the clay gently to remove the ball. Smooth the inside of the candle holder with your fingers or a damp sponge – this area won't have dried yet, so we can add some detail or texture. I have used the end of a paintbrush and marked on some grooves.

10. Place the correct way up and leave to dry fully.

11. Once completely dry, sand any rough areas as necessary. Paint the inside of the holder with a light colour paint, then give a second coat if needed. Choose a contrasting colour and paint the outside of the clay holder, up to the sharp edge of the rim. Seal to protect; I used a gloss acrylic varnish.

12. Add tealights as a beautiful decoration for the home.

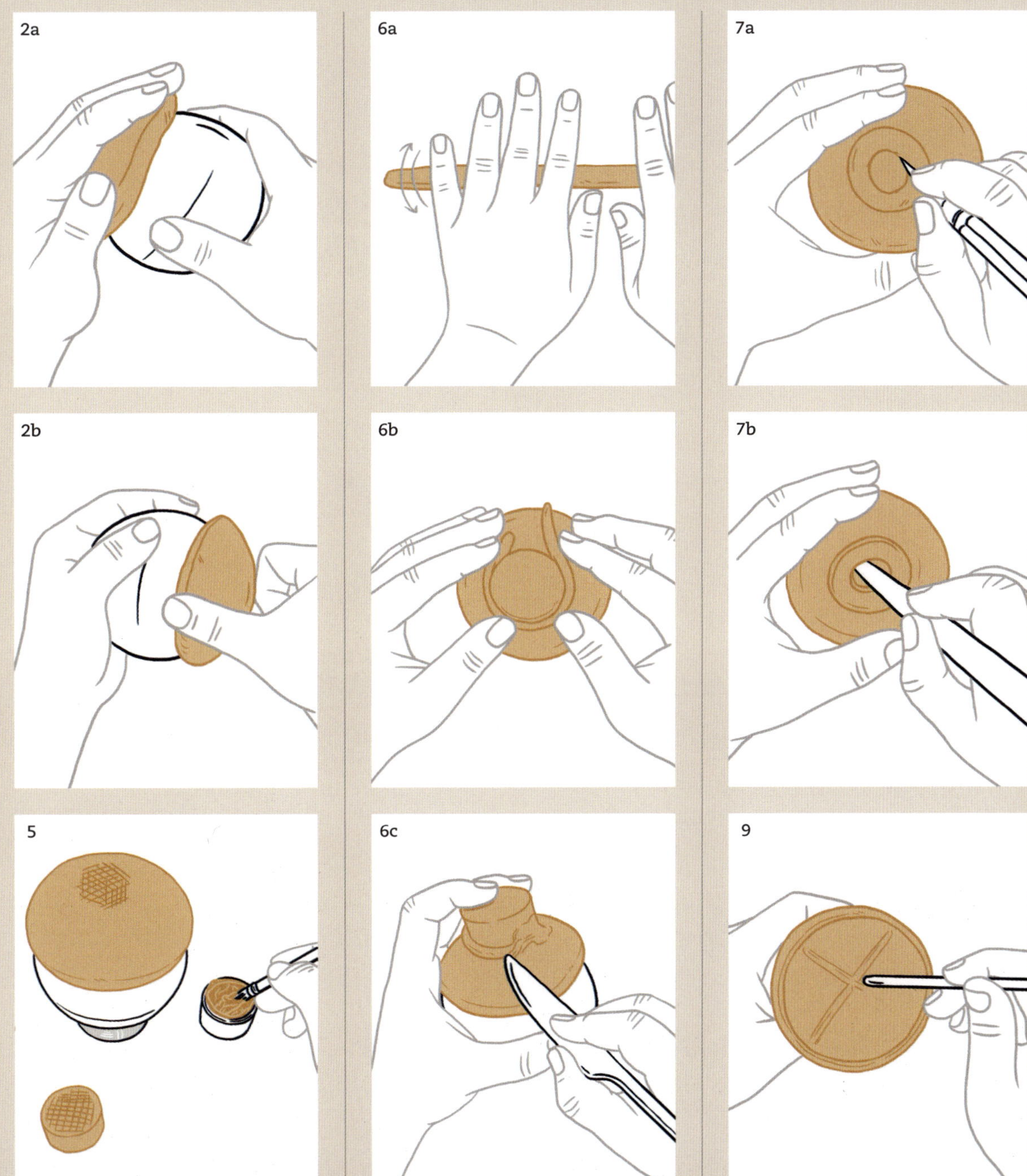
2a
6a
7a
2b
6b
7b
5
6c
9

TEXTURED CLOCK

I love adding texture and dimension to clay, and the texture on this piece is easy to achieve, with pleasing results. If smoothing clay to perfection is not your style, then adding texture really might be. In this (quite large) project I create a simple, contemporary clock from air-dry clay and add texture with sand and pepper.

WHAT YOU NEED

Clock mechanism, box measuring approx. 60 x 60 x 15mm (2⅜ x 2⅜ x ½in)
1kg (2.2lb) air-dry clay
Paper template (see p.138)
Sand/coarsely ground pepper
Rolling pin
Knife/scalpel
Drinking straw
Parchment paper (or similar non-stick surface)
Sharp implement, e.g. toothpick
Spray varnish/sealant (matt spray lacquer is an option)

1. Sprinkle your work surface with some sand (I used children's play sand). Begin to roll out your clay on this surface, aiming for the size of your paper template.

2. Before the clay has reached the size of the template, sprinkle the top of the clay with some sand, and some coarsely ground pepper if you wish. Keep rolling until the template fits easily on the clay, taking care not to roll any thinner than 10mm (⅜in). Some of the sand and pepper will come loose, but you will notice it also leaves a lovely texture. If you would like to add extra texture, you can take a crumpled piece of tin foil and indent the clay all over with a dabbing motion.

3. Place the template onto the clay, hold in position and cut the shape out. Mark the position of the clock mechanism on the clay and set the template to one side.

4. Tap the edges of the clay into shape if required and also tap some sand onto the edges with your fingers. Take a straw and cut a hole where the clock mechanism will fit into the clay (marked in step 3).

DECORATION SUGGESTION

As an alternative to the sandy texture, this piece could have a smooth finish and be painted with bold colours and patterns. I personally would not paint over the sand texture – it could get a bit messy!

TIP

These larger items gain strength from varnishing, but still need to be looked after and not knocked, just as if they were made of ceramic.

5. Gently turn the clay over and set aside on a tile or piece of parchment paper. You'll hopefully notice that the sand prevents the clay from sticking to the surface.

6. Form the remaining clay into a long coil and roll this out to the length of the clock base. Use a knife/ruler to cut the piece that will form the clock stand (260 x 60 x 10mm/10¼ x 2⅜ x ⅜in). This will be the support that lies flat when the clock is upright.

7. Use the score and slip method (p.20) to join these two slabs together at the base.

8. Roll and add a long, thin coil of clay to the inside of the join, blending and joining the two slabs together. This extra step gives further, much needed strength.

9. I added an indent to the back of the clock where the mechanism sits using the mechanism itself. Make sure the moving parts will protrude enough at the front of the clock so that the hands can be added.

10. Leave to dry with a block of wood or similar propping up the stand at a 90-degree angle. Turn the clock onto the stand after some time drying, and dry in this position.

11. Once fully dry, spray with varnish. I like to use a matt varnish on sand – don't worry if some flecks drop out. Once this is dry, add a second coat if you feel the sand needs to be further secured,

12. Insert the clock mechanism and a battery, to get your clock ticking!

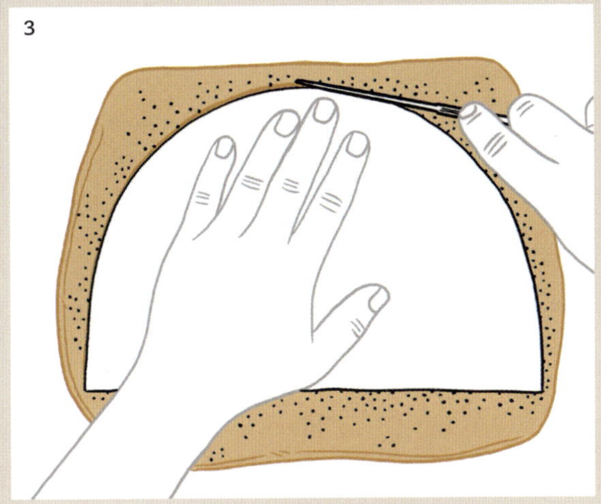
3

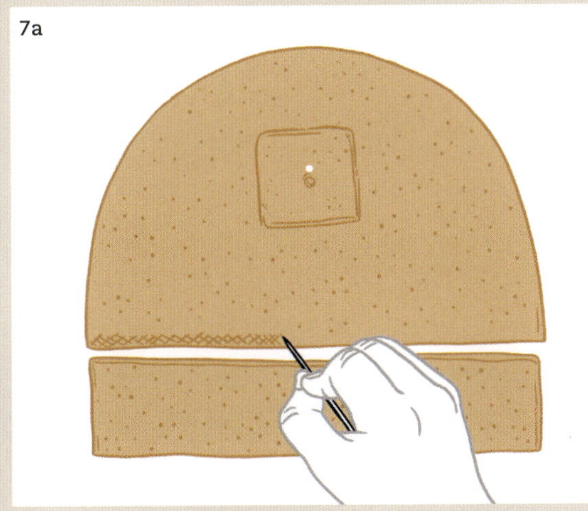
7a

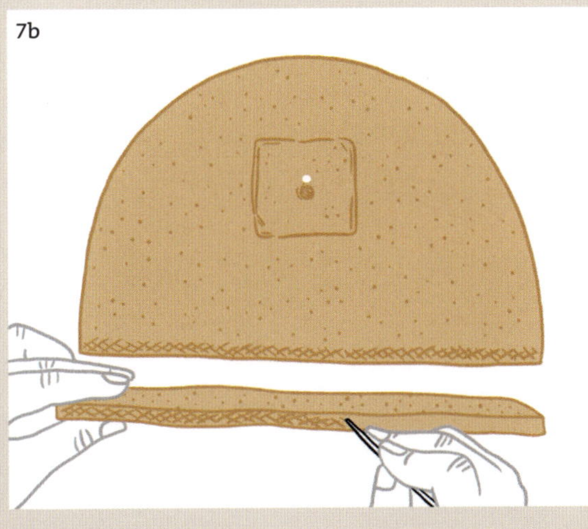
7b

8

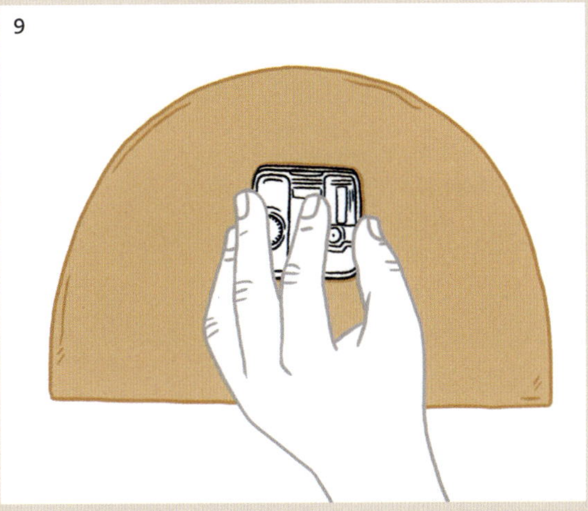
9

HANGING PLANT POT

This project is a perfectly practical item and will teach you the pinch pot technique. The basic form can then be adapted to create many other shapes. I love the contrast between the colour and texture and the smooth white – it is simple but effective.

WHAT YOU NEED

250g (8.8oz) air-dry clay
Drinking straw
Paintbrush
Sandpaper
Paint (watercolour or acrylic)
Sealant
3m (10ft) string/twine/ thin rope
Plant

Optional

Sponge
Shallow plastic container

TIP

Air-dry clay will turn to mush if it has water sitting in it for long periods of time. Always protect and seal your projects, and add an internal vessel if water is going to sit within.

1. Make your air-dry clay into a nice smooth ball.

2. Hold the clay in your non-dominant hand and press the thumb of your other hand into the centre of the clay ball.

3. Creating a paddle with your fingers, use a pinching motion to shape the clay as you rotate the ball, working around the sides. If any cracks appear, smooth them out, and if it starts to dry, just add the smallest amount of water or slip (p.19) to your fingers. Keep repeating, squeezing between your thumb and fingers, and turning, until you have a semisphere of clay with a hole in the centre; the walls should be 8–10mm (⅜in) in thickness or slightly thicker.

4. Turn the pot upside down and encourage the clay to form a flat rim against the flat surface of your board. Smooth out the pot shape as necessary; I used a small damp sponge to do this.

5. Make three evenly spaced holes near the top rim of the pot using a drinking straw. These will be used to hang the planter, so make sure the holes are at least 12mm (½in) from the edge.

6. Smooth the clay with a small amount of water or slip.

7. To give the clay some texture, use the end of a large paintbrush and make some dimples in the clay. The pattern is completely up to you – experiment, and enjoy the creative process. Don't worry if small cracks appear in the outer surface of the clay during this process – this is hard to avoid in air-dry clay. I personally love the added character that the tiny crinkles give to the piece.

8. Do any last bits of smoothing and then turn the pot upside down and leave to dry. After a while, turn the clay the right side up to help with drying, and repeat if necessary.

9. Once fully dry, you can lightly sand the pot with sandpaper if needed and paint. Leave to dry.

10. Seal the clay. I used a spray varnish on this one, as it made it easy to get into all the crevices. For the inside of the pot, I sometimes add a shallow plastic container, to catch any leaked water, or you can add resin or polyurethane varnish in the base.

11. Use some string or thin rope to hang. I used three double stands, gathered together and tied at the top.

12. Hang and admire.

DECORATION SUGGESTION

You can paint with acrylic paints or, as I have on this occasion, use watercolour paints (the white section at the top was painted with white acrylic) – these give a lovely natural vibe. Once dry, I sealed the watercolour with an all-in-one glue-like sealant – something like a decoupage medium – as this doesn't seem to re-activate the watercolours. A different varnish can then be added over the whole piece.

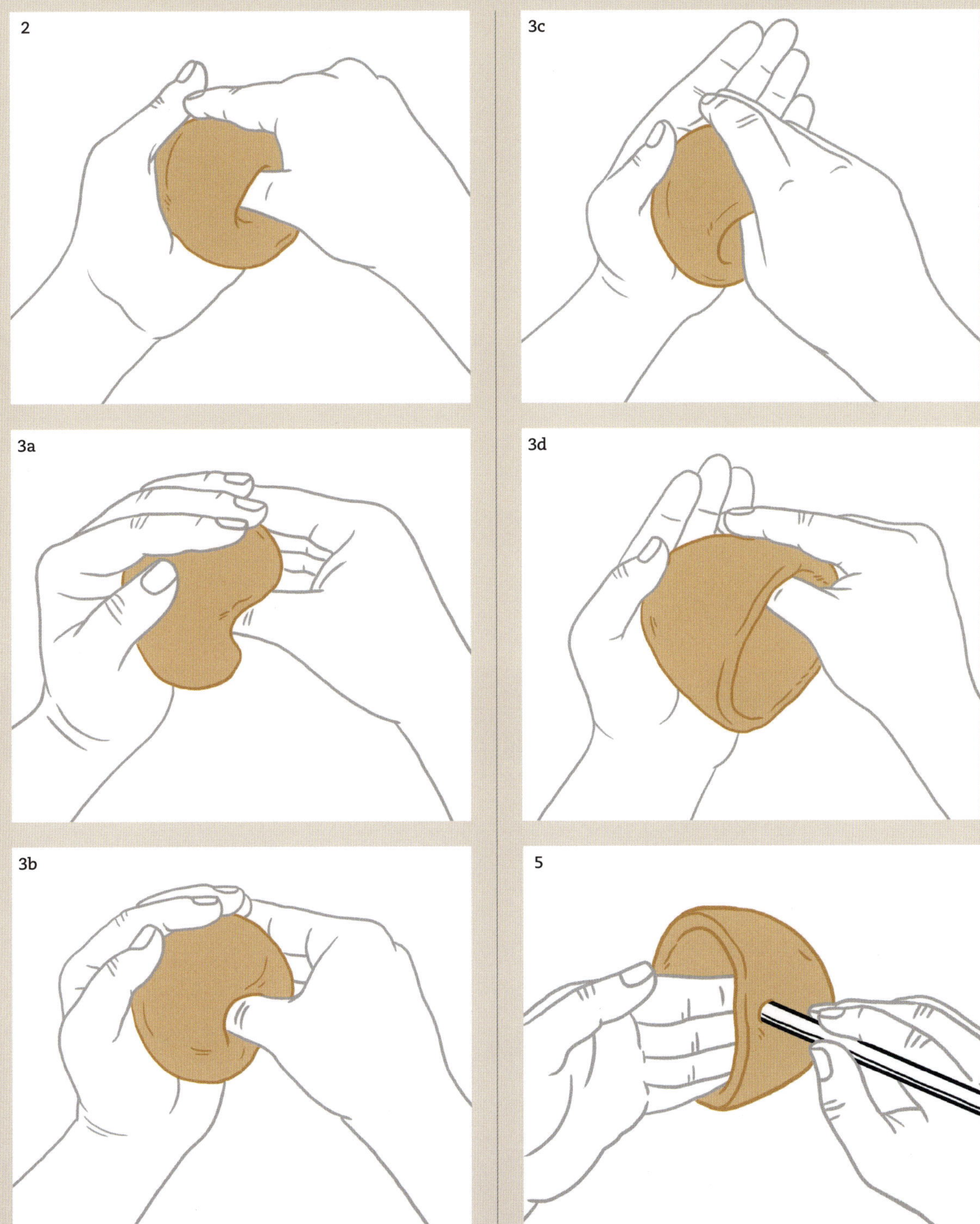
2
3a
3b
3c
3d
5

TISSUE BOX COVER

Tissue boxes aren't very pretty to look at, so this cover is the perfect solution. The form may be simple, but the simplest pieces are often excellent for perfecting a technique, especially when you have a few little tricks up your sleeve... Decoration techniques like these 'bubbles' make all the difference.

WHAT YOU NEED

1kg (2.2lb) air-dry clay
Tissue box
Corrugated cardboard
Scissors
Masking tape
Cling film
Knife
Metal ruler
Drinking straw or similar
Paint
Sealant

1. I use the tissue box as a mould for this simple design. Temporarily cover the top and sides of the tissue box with one layer of corrugated cardboard, cutting neatly to size with scissors and taping in place. Cover the whole surface with cling film; tape in place if necessary.

2. On a large surface, roll out the whole piece of clay to approximately 8–10mm (⅜in) in thickness.

3. Place the covered box in the centre of the clay. Using a knife or metal ruler, cut a straight line down the two opposite short sides of the box. Remove the box.

4. Using the ruler, measure and mark the centre point of the clay. Around this central point, mark a rectangle measuring 120 x 10mm (4¾ x ⅜in) on the clay – this is where the tissue will come out when the cover is complete. I like to take a wide straw (or a round paint-brush sleeve or pen lid) and use this to cut the short ends of the rectangle, and then, with a knife, cut the longer straight edges. Remove the clay and smooth the gap.

5. Gently lift the clay sheet over the box so that the edges line up neatly and the slit is where you want it, in the centre of the box. Smooth this clay slab down and use a knife or ruler to trim off the excess on the two long sides.

6. Take a ruler and measure the ends of the box where there is no clay. Note the dimensions down, or make a paper template from them.

7. Gather and knead the remaining clay, then roll out to 8–10mm (⅜in) in thickness. Using a ruler or the template, cut out two rectangles to the measurements taken in the previous step.

8. Using the score and slip technique (p.20), add the rectangles of clay to each end of the box. I then rolled a 6mm (¼in) coil of clay, added slip to the joins and molded the coils in place to make the joins much stronger.

9. Leave to dry for a few hours with the box inside. Once it has started to firm up, turn the whole project over and gently remove the tissue box, cardboard and cling film. Smooth the internal joints at this point. Make sure the sides are still straight and leave to dry upside down. Once it is almost completely dry, finish the drying the right way up, making sure the tissue box still fits inside.

10. Paint and seal. I used a gloss acrylic varnish.

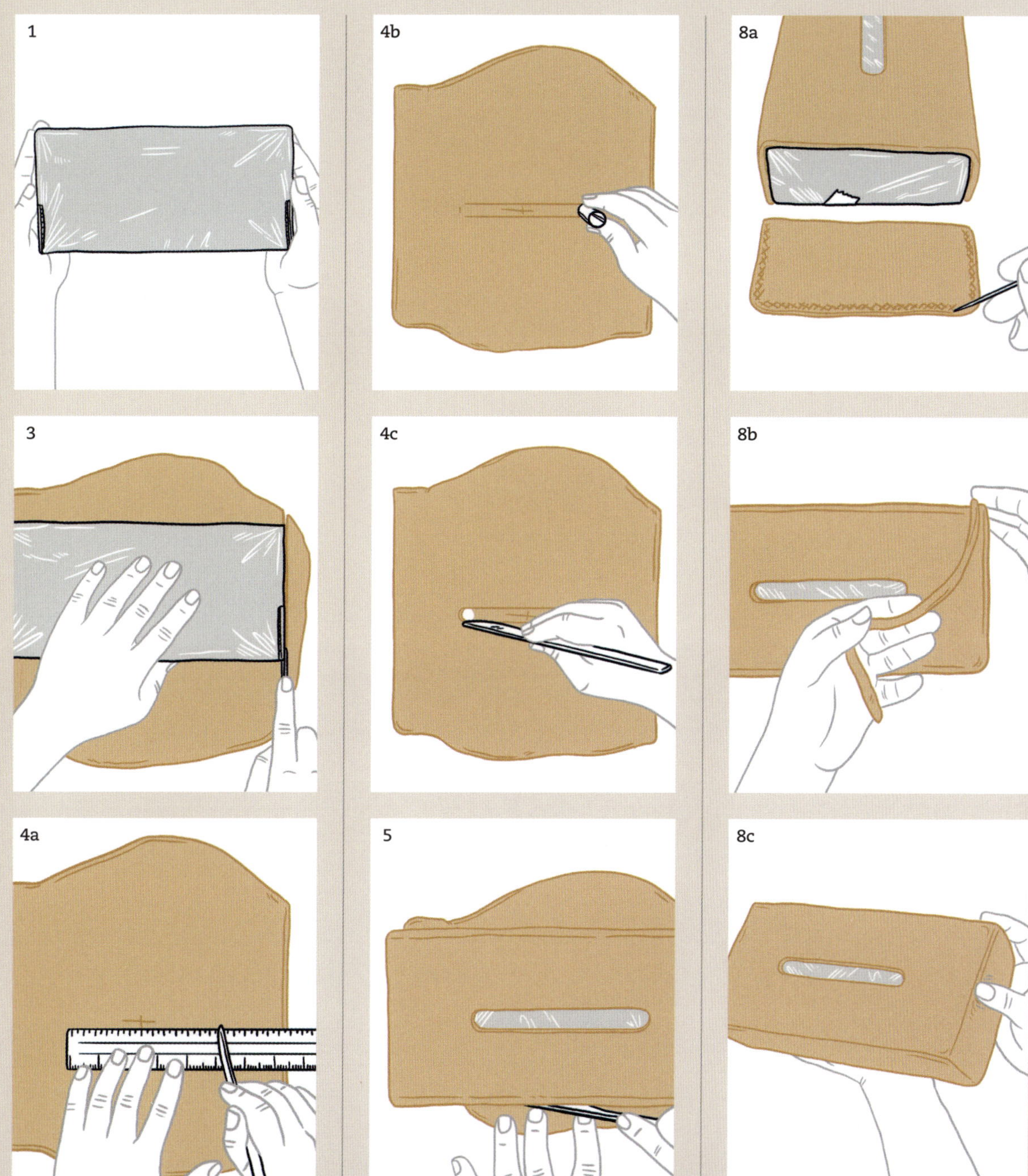
1
3
4a
4b
4c
5
8a
8b
8c

3a

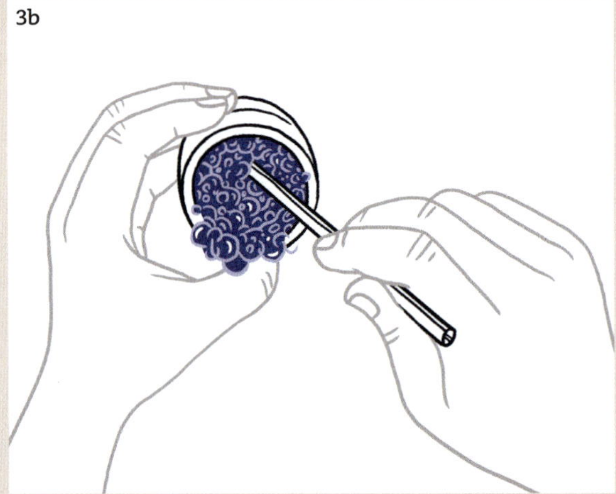
3b

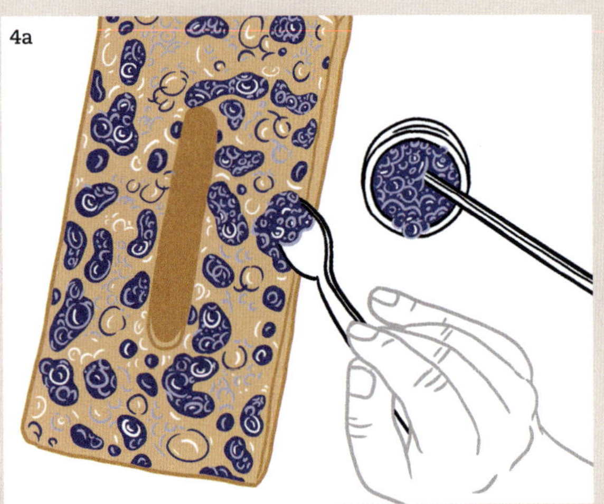
4a

4b

DECORATION SUGGESTION

1. I added a fun 'bubble' finish to this piece. I started by painting the inside and outside of the box with blue acrylic paint. The next part is fairly messy, so cover all surfaces and clothes.

2. To make the bubble mixture, combine 1 teaspoon of acrylic paint with 1 teaspoon of dish soap in a tall-sided plastic cup, and then add 4 teaspoons of water, mixing thoroughly.

3. Put a drinking straw to the bottom of the cup and gently start to blow out to form bubbles – this definitely takes me back to being a child! Bubbles will start to make their way up the cup; knock them back to start with and keep blowing the bubbles, as this encourages lots of tiny bubbles and not just big ones.

4. After about 30 seconds allow the bubbles to come up the cup. Either allow them to come up and over the sides and onto the clay (a bit of aim is required), or lift them out with a spoon – just the bubbles, not the excess bubble mixture at the base of the cup.

5. I like to work on one surface at a time, allowing it to dry before turning to the next one. You can see a demonstration of these bubbles on my Red Rocking Bird YouTube channel. If you would like to add another colour, you can do this once the first layer is dry.

6. Seal. I used a gloss acrylic varnish

TIP

The thinner the straw, the finer the bubbles, so experiment and lose yourself in this wonderfully creative project!

TIP

I recommend trying a new technique, like the bubbles, on a small piece of clay first, so that you have had a practice before you go straight onto a piece you have spent quite some time creating. But don't worry if you don't like the finished result. You can always paint over with acrylic paint and try again.

WALL-HANGING FLOWER POCKET

This is a project I am sure you will want to repeat, once you realize how straightforward it is. One hung up on a wall or a collection of various shapes and sizes all hung together all look beautiful. Don't worry if you can't get your clay lovely and smooth; you could add some texture, or a stone effect like I give the Little Bird Cottonbud Caddy (pp.115–17). I always say, work to your strengths and what works for you. Cut some clay and begin!

WHAT YOU NEED

500g (17.6oz) air-dry clay
Rolling pin or similar
Knife
Drinking straw
Sandpaper
Paint
Sealant
50mm (2in) string/ribbon
Dried flowers

Optional

Sponge

1. Roll the air-dry clay to 8mm (⅜in) in thickness.

2. I like to cut a freehand rectangle with my knife – about 130 x 170mm (5⅛ x 6¾in), rounded and slightly tapered at the top. I personally enjoy the organic, more unusual shapes that can be created this way. But if you prefer to follow a template then I have included one for you on p.140.

3. Cut a smaller rectangle – approx. 65 x 80mm (2½ x 3⅛in) – with a straight top edge and curved corners at the bottom (again there is a template on p.141). Remove all excess clay from the edges and store for later.

4. Place the small rectangle of clay on top of the larger piece of clay (the template also contains a guide for this placement) and press down slightly. Lift the small rectangle off to reveal a light indent.

5. Score and add slip to the 'U' shape indent. Do the same to the back of the small rectangle.

6. Place the small rectangle back on top of the larger piece and press the sides down. Use your fingers to encourage the 'pocket' shape of the top piece. If you find it easier, you could cut a sponge to size and place this inside the little pocket to ensure it holds its shape.

7. Smooth the edges of the small rectangle completely, using a knife to blend the edges together. Then you can get some air-dry clay slip on your fingers and smooth out the join until it disappears. Smooth the whole piece (or add texture).

8. Use a drinking straw to make two holes at the top of the piece, as shown on the previous page.

9. Leave to dry. You will need to leave this lying flat to dry until the pocket is dry – only then can it be turned to dry the underside. This ensures the final piece can hang flat on a wall.

10. Once dry, sand as required.

11. This kind of piece could be painted in white acrylic paint without any detail, and then sealed, to let the flowers stand out, especially if you have added texture. Or decorate, as I have, using acrylic paints to create a contemporary feel.

12. Seal. I used a matt, water-based varnish. Once the sealant is dry, thread the ribbon or string through the two holes and hang on a nail or from a shelf to display dried flowers.

TIP

If you had something like a plastic or glass test tube, the pocket could 'house' this vessel. Wrap a piece of card, and then cling film, around the tube while the clay dries in the correct shape, then remove. Once the piece is fully dry, you can add the tube back in and this would allow you to add water and fresh flowers to the vase.

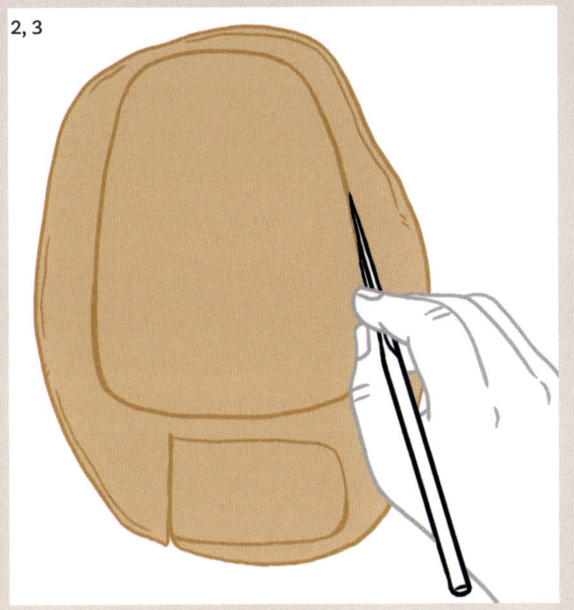
2, 3

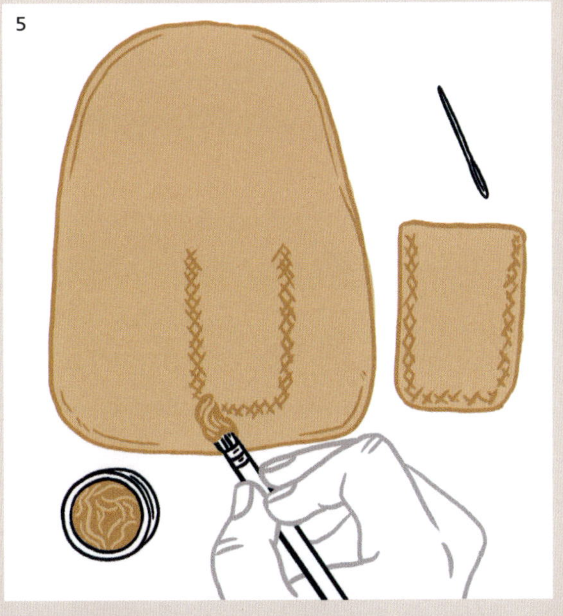
5

7

CANDLESTICK HOLDER

Displaying candles in the home creates a really cosy and warm ambience. This piece features a dish so that you can place a matchbox or lighter near your candles, and it could also serve as a trinket dish. Festive seasons call for beautiful items like this, and any simple shape can be created using this coiled-edge method.

WHAT YOU NEED

500g (17.6oz) air-dry clay
Candles
Rolling pin
Paper template
Knife or scalpel
Round-ended knife
Thin card
Sticking tape
Toothpick
Paintbrush
Sandpaper
Paint
Sealant

Optional

Sponge

1. Create a paper template for the base of the candlestick holder; the heart I have used is included at the back of the book (p.137).

2. Roll the clay to 8mm (⅜in) in thickness and cut out the shape for the base.

3. Knead the remaining clay back together and then into a long coil 15mm (½in) in diameter and 500mm (19⅝in) in length, trying to keep it as even as possible all the way along. This will form the walls of the candle dish (so you may need to make it to a different length if you choose a different shape for the base).

4. Score the outer 15mm (½in) of the heart shape and add some air-dry clay slip (p.19). Place the long coil on top of the scored area, all the way around the perimeter of the heart, and press down firmly.

5. Using the joining method, bring the clay from the bottom up on the outside of the dish, using a rounded knife to make it easier, and smooth everything over.

6. Join the clay on the inside of the coil, also, using a rounded knife to pull the clay down from the coil onto the inside of the dish.

7. Smooth everything over with your finger/brush/sponge and some air-dry clay slip.

8. Wrap the base of your candle with some thin card, taped in place.

9. Roll the remaining clay to 8mm ($\frac{3}{8}$in) in thickness and cut a 42mm- ($1\frac{5}{8}$in-) wide rectangle to fit around the base of your candle.

10. Gently wrap the base of the candle with the rectangle of clay and cut where the ends meet. Use the score, slip and coil method (pp.19–20) to join these edges. Remove the candle and smooth.

11. Place the loop of clay created in step 10 onto the heart dish where you would like it attached. Use a toothpick to mark this positioning, scoring a line around the loop.

TIP

Make sure the wick of your candle doesn't get too low – the candle flame shouldn't come into contact with the clay, so as not to create a fire hazard or damage the piece.

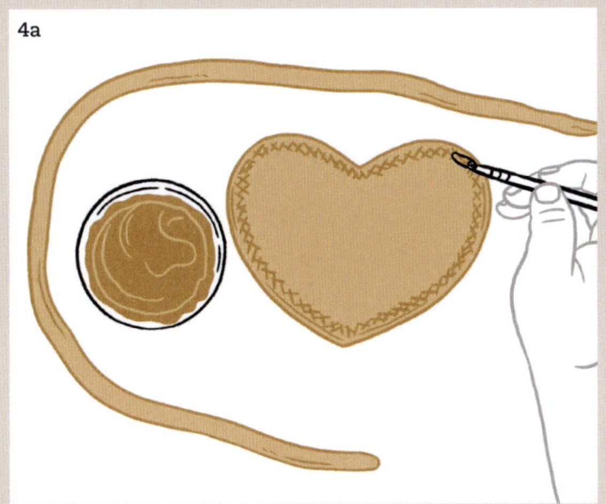
4a

4b

5

6

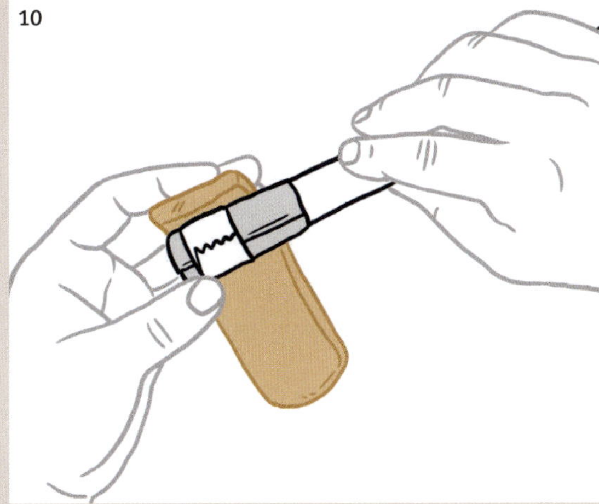
10

12. Score and slip the loop in place. I blended the clay downwards towards the dish and then added a 7mm (¼in) coil around the base to give a strong structure. My knife was too big to blend this in place, so I used the rounded end of a paintbrush to blend and smooth.

13. Smooth everything out with some air-dry clay slip.

14. Put the candle back into the clay loop to check it still fits and make sure everything is vertical.

15. Allow to dry fully.

16. Sand, paint and seal. I used acrylic paint and a gloss acrylic varnish.

DECORATION SUGGESTION

I gave the whole piece two coats of white acrylic paint. I added a little water to some blue acrylic paint then tapped the loaded paintbrush on a pencil to add flecks of paint all over the piece. If you would like to do this over just part of a piece, then you can cover up an area with low-tack masking tape and peel the tape off once the flecks have dried.

12a

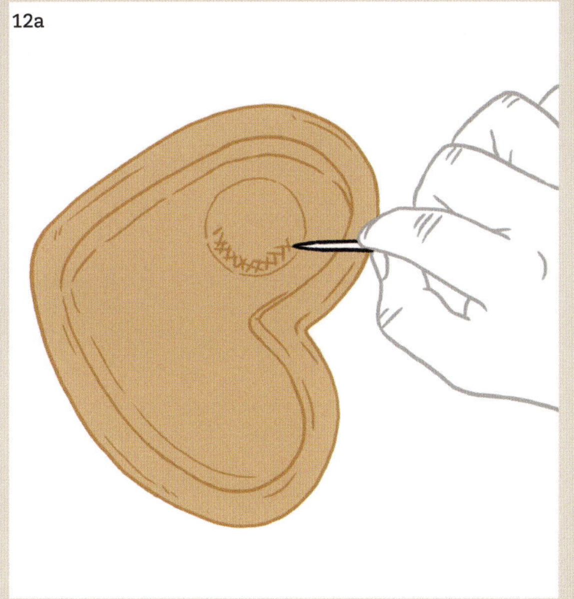

12b

12c

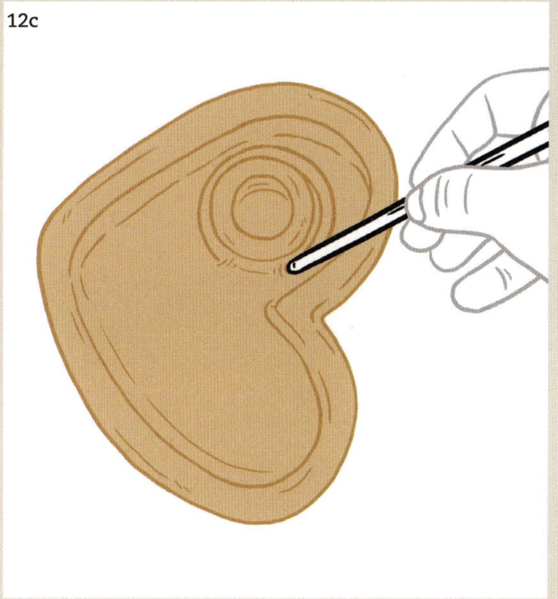

16

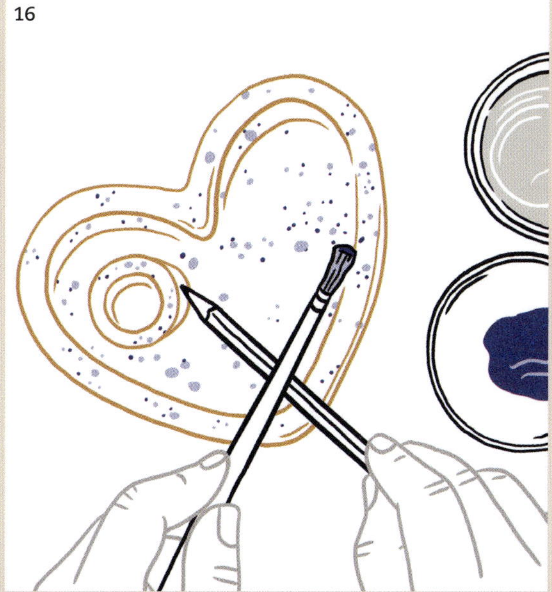

Decoration Suggestion

CHAPTER 3

MASTERING AIR-DRY CLAY

Working through this section of the book, you can add to your skills with air-dry clay. Experiment even further with different ways to colour and decorate the clay. The introduction of armatures (support structures within the clay) allows us to build larger pieces with a broader range of shapes.

I am full to the brim with ideas of things to make from air-dry clay, so I hope this book is inspiring you and that you are feeling more confident with your clay projects. Keep trying, keep learning and really enjoy the creativity that this medium offers you.

BUD VASE

I absolutely love the little technique that I use to make these cute vases. The idea is to use a pencil or a wooden dowel as an 'internal' rolling pin – try it out and see what you think. Once you have mastered the technique, experiment with different quantities of clay.

In this project I also introduce you to marbling clay. This creates a gorgeous pattern, and means you don't have to think about painting your finished piece. If you want to try this out, marble your clay before you start building your vase.

WHAT YOU NEED

100g (3½oz) air-dry clay
Pencil or wooden dowel, at least 200mm (7⅞in) in length
Scalpel/knife
Paintbrushes
Sandpaper
Acrylic paint
Sealant

Optional

Sponge

1. Between the palms of your hands or against the table, roll the clay into a thick coil approximately 120mm (4¾in) long, with an even thickness and flattened ends. The final vase will be approximately this tall and a little wider.

2. Smooth out any cracks with some air-dry clay slip on your fingers, or use a sponge if preferred.

3. Take the pencil or wooden dowel and push this into the very centre of one end of the clay coil, trying to keep it as central as possible. Hold the clay firmly but not so firmly that you make indents in the clay with your fingers. I find that turning the clay helps me keep the pencil/dowel central as I push it until it protrudes through the opposite end. If you find you're going off track, then take the pencil/dowel out a little and reposition.

4. Place the clay on a smooth surface and put a hand on each side of the pencil/dowel. Press down lightly and roll forward and back a few times. The hole in the clay will gradually widen as you roll around the inside of the clay. The clay wall should be about 8mm (⅜in) thick (thicker if you wish, which would result in a slimmer vase).

5. Tap the end that you choose to be the base against a table to flatten it out a little.

6. With a knife, trim the top of the vase to a neat edge, removing at least 5g (⅛oz) of clay. Flatten this remnant of clay to a disc just a little smaller than the diameter of the vase.

7. Use the score and slip method (p.20) to attach the disc to the bottom of the bud vase. Smooth.

8. Stand upright and leave to dry.

9. Sand, decorate, seal (I used a gloss acrylic varnish) and add dried flowers.

DECORATION SUGGESTION

Try your hand at marbling the clay before you start. Take two colours of air-dry clay; I am using both white and stone. Roll 50g (1¾oz) of each colour to form two coils, then place the two coils together and twist. Roll on your surface into a longer coil, then fold in half, twist and roll again, pressing the clay together firmly. Do this as many times as you wish. The less you twist the bolder the pattern will be; more twists make for a subtler pattern.

If at any time you feel the clay is drying out, then add a bit of air-dry clay slip to your fingers and encourage the clay together.

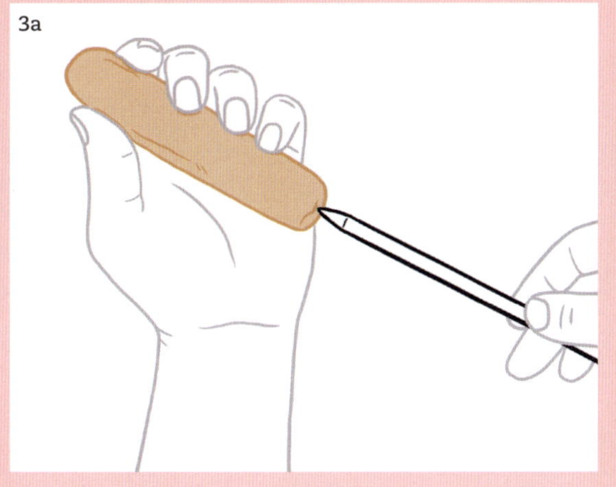

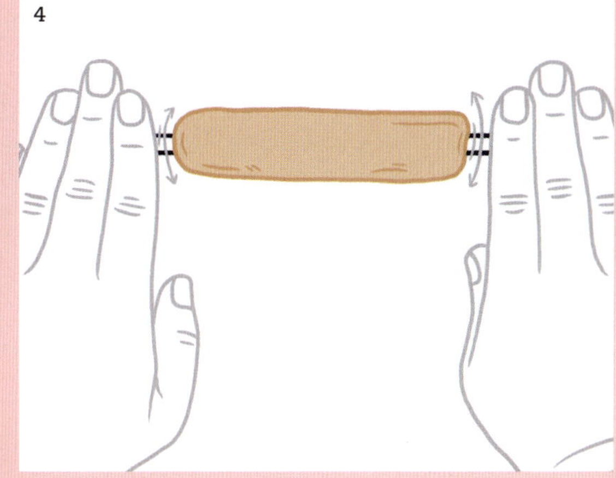

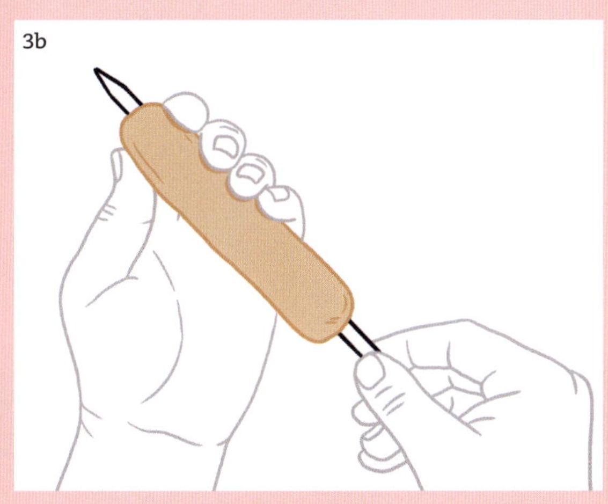

Decoration Suggestion

PEN POT

This pot uses the slab building technique. While it is perfect for storing pens and paintbrushes, you could also use it as a vase for dried flowers. With a vessel inside, one of these pots could also hold water and fresh flowers.

WHAT YOU NEED

600g (21⅛oz) air-dry clay
Rolling pin
Round cookie cutter, 110mm (4⅜in) in diameter
A4 card
Scissors
Knife/scalpel
Ruler
Toothpick or similar
Round-edged knife
Paintbrushes
Acrylic paint
Sealant
Sandpaper

Optional

Sponge

TIP

As a beginner, it is easier to create thicker, shorter walls, as these are easier to handle – make the height of your cup something more like 60mm (2⅜in).

1. As this project is made using the slab building technique, we first cut slabs for the base and the walls. First, take approximately 150g (5¼oz) of clay and roll to 10mm (⅜in) in thickness. Cut a disc from this using the 110mm (4⅜in) cookie cutter.

2. Form all the remaining clay into a coil that is approximately 300mm (12in) long, ready for step 4.

3. Using the piece of card, measure the circumference of the clay disc. Then cut the card to size for your pot sides; for a 110mm (4⅜in) disc, the circumference is approximately 350mm (13¾in). Cut the card to the height you would like (mine is 95mm (3¾in) high. Set the clay disc aside.

4. Roll the clay coil out to 10mm (⅜in) in thickness, making sure you roll the clay as long as your piece of card. Using the card as a template, cut the clay to size.

5. Take a toothpick or sharp pointed tool and add score marks (score and slip technique, p.20) to the edge of the disc and bottom, cut edge of the rectangle. Paste a thin layer of air-dry clay slip onto these score marks.

6. Make sure the round disc is on a tile or work surface that can be moved, as it will remain here while it dries. Lift the rectangle with the score marks facing downward and align these marks with the score marks of the disc. If the long piece of clay overlaps at each end, cut down through the sides at an angle with a knife. Score and slip this edge together, and smooth.

7. Start to attach the disc to the sides with a blunt knife, blending the join by pulling the clay up from the work surface and past the join. Work all around the base.

8. Add some slip to the internal joins. Roll some of the remaining clay into a long, 5mm- (⅛in-) wide coil. Place this on the internal joins and blend into the clay walls until they disappear, strengthening the join.

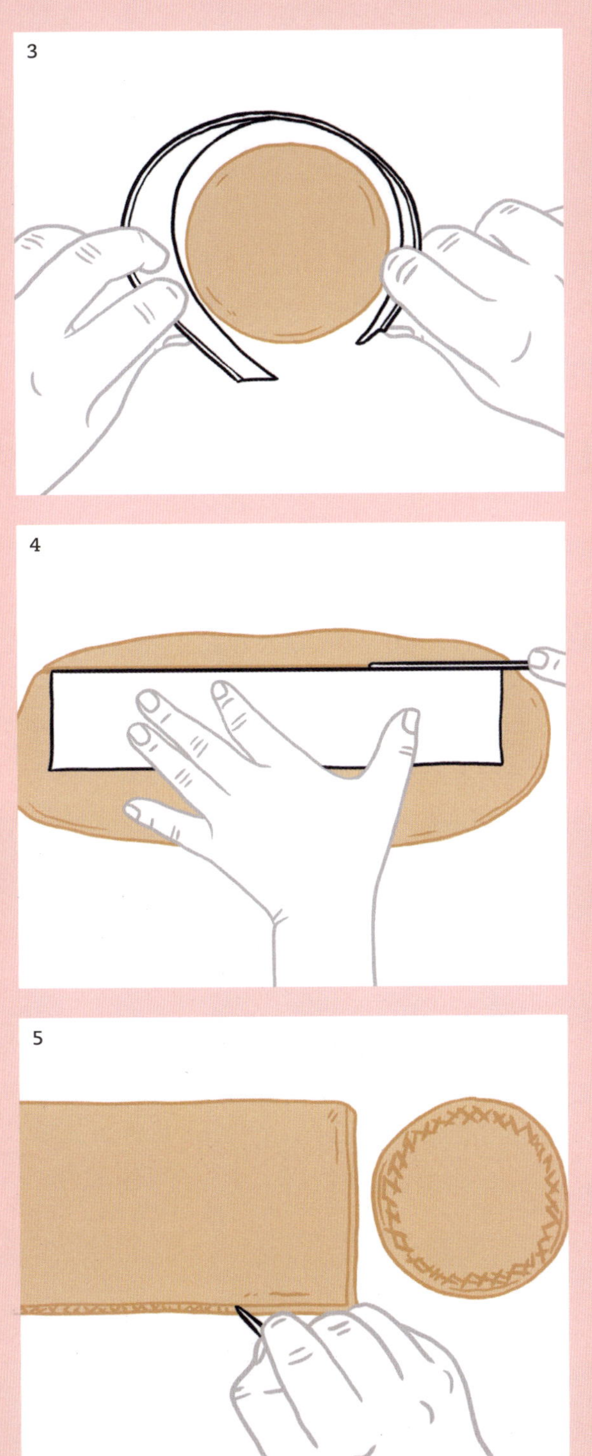
3
4
5

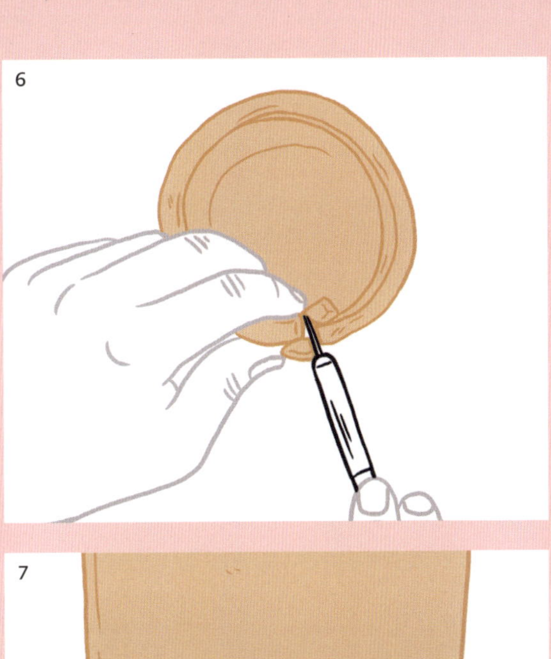
6

7

TIP

A wine glass held upside down and placed very gently into the opening of the pot can help re-shape the opening. Turn the glass gently and lift it away.

9. If the overall shape of the pot has distorted at all, now is a good time to reshape with your fingers. I also smooth the top lip of the pot to give a rounded edge. Use air-dry clay slip on your fingers, or a sponge.

10. Use clay offcuts to make a 'handle' (this is decorative, and should not actually be used to lift the pot). I have used a heart-shaped cookie cutter to cut one for this design; you can also use the template on p.139 and cut the clay with a knife or scalpel.

11. With the score and slip and coil method (p.20) attach the heart to the pot. It is important to support the weight of the 'handle' while this join dries, otherwise it is likely to fall off. Smooth any indents one last time before leaving to dry.

12. Once this has been drying for a day or two and has started to firm up, gently twist and lift the pot from the surface and turn over to allow the base to dry (on books, with the heart overhanging the edge). Allow to dry fully.

13. Once dry, sand with sandpaper as required. Paint and seal. I used acrylic paint and a matt varnish.

DECORATION SUGGESTION

I painted the whole inside and outside of the pot in a light-grey acrylic paint, then the bottom third in a darker grey. Once this base was dry, I added the white dots, a yellow heart and black line with a flat brush. To create the straight black line, I rested my pencil on top of the cookie cutter and turned the pot slowly, allowing the pencil to run straight around the pot. I then used a size-0 paintbrush to paint over the line.

BOOKEND

This project teaches you how to create a simple 3D form and is a good example of how to create heavier objects from air-dry clay. Using this technique you can create so many different designs. Bear in mind that this is a decorative piece that can hold up a few books, but not a whole bookshelf of heavy books.

WHAT YOU NEED

1kg (2.2lb) air-dry clay
Large stone/pebble
Full reel of craft wire, approx. 8+ gauge
Tin foil
Round-edged knife
Sandpaper
Paint
Sealant

Optional

Hot glue

1. Wrap the stone with the wire, so that it is securely held. The stone will be at the base of the bookend to keep the weight low. Extend the wire upwards to form a lovely curve on each side. Use the photograph opposite as a guide – the dimensions are up to you, depending on the size of your books.

2. Scrunch some tin foil into a thick disc and sit the stone on top of this as the base. Scrunch some more tin foil and pad out the area above the stone, to start to form a curve.

3. Rip off long sections of tin foil – scrunch them up then unscrunch them. This scrunching gives the foil some 'body' and something for the clay to grip on to. Start to wrap the structure with the foil, adding more until you have the size you require. Loop it around the wire securely. You can use hot glue to help with this. Also take a couple of larger scrunched sheets and wrap the stone, so that everything is fully covered in foil. The aim is to make the form that you want to end up with, minus approximately 8mm (⅜in) in thickness.

4. Roll half of the clay out to 8mm (⅜in) in thickness.

5. Use the clay to start covering a large section of the tin-foil structure – I like to start with the largest part, so the lower section. Make a cut on each side of the clay to allow it to bend around the structure.

6. Take some more flattened clay and add this over any uncovered areas of tin foil, then smooth and blend the seams together. Keep repeating this over the whole piece – you can do this in smaller or larger sections of clay, whichever you prefer. I often use a blunt table knife to help join and smooth the edges, using some air-dry clay slip, too, especially if it is drying out. Really use your hands to sculpt the shape, leaving one side slightly flatter so that it can support books.

TIP

When using a stone in this way, always make sure it is clean, and allow it to dry fully in a warm spot for a few days before using. If the stone contains moisture on the inside, it will take the clay even longer to dry. I learned this the hard way!

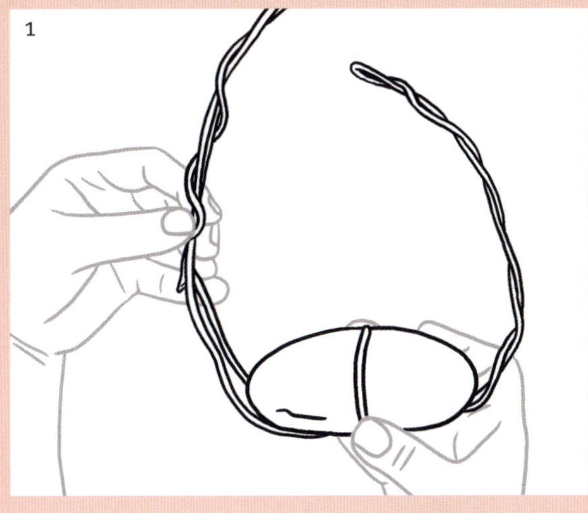
1

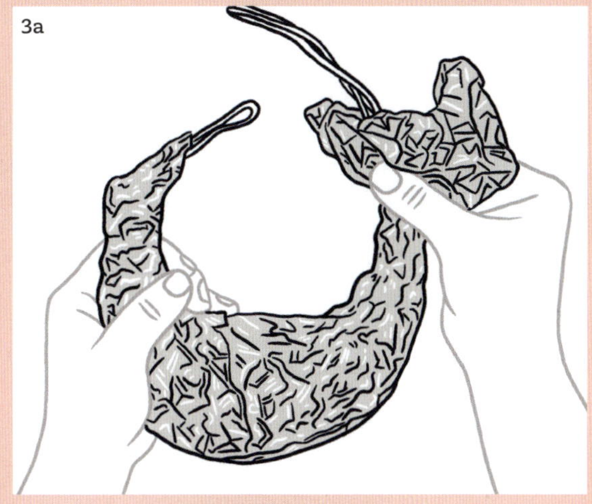
3a

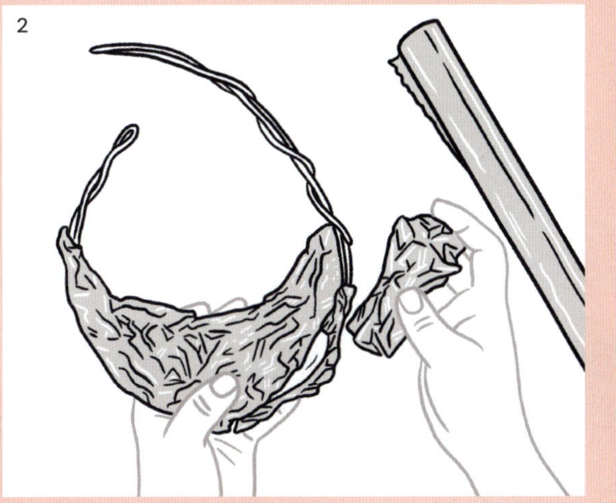
2

3b

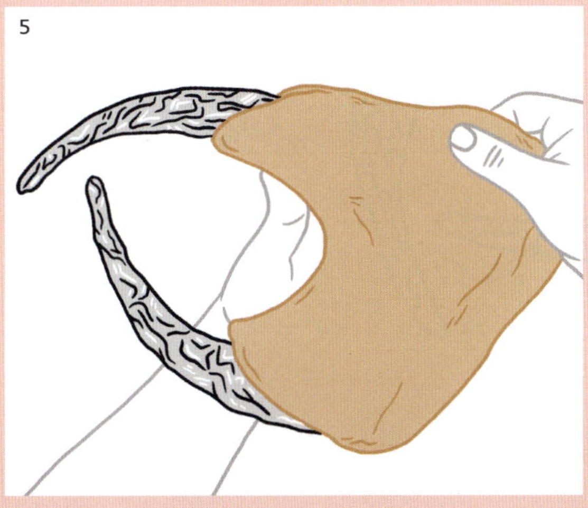
5

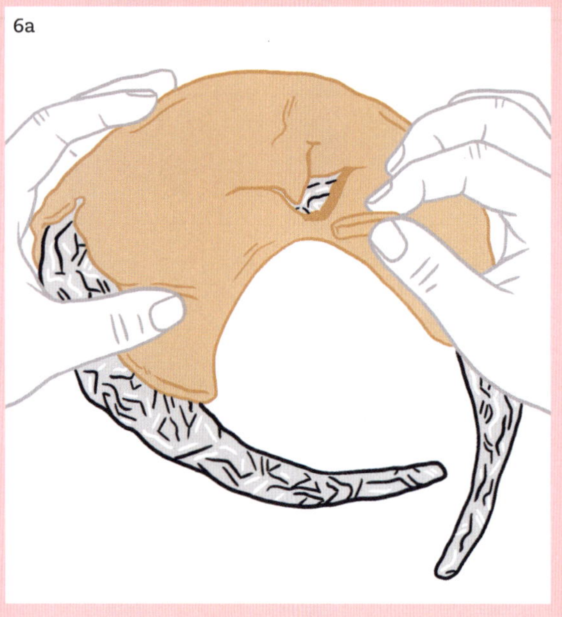
6a

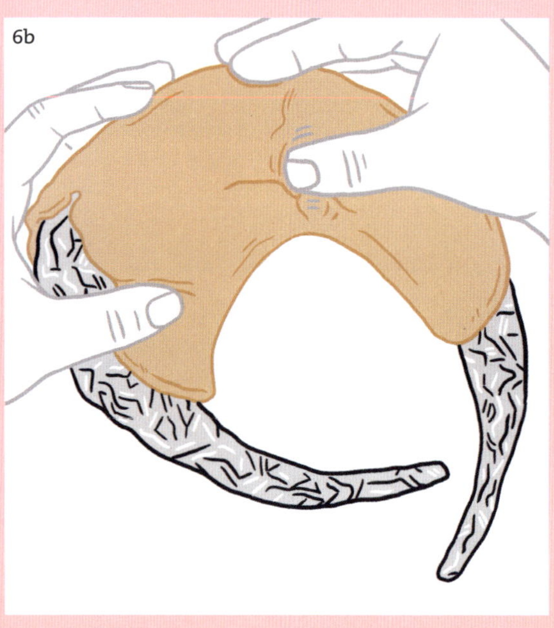
6b

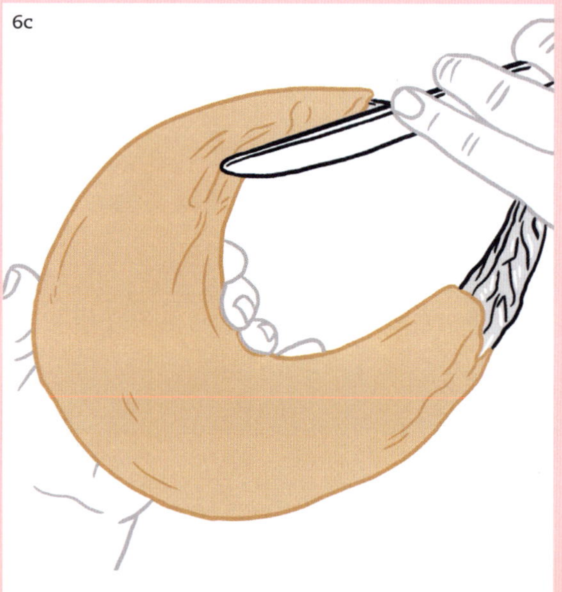
6c

7. The beauty of this design it that it doesn't have to be too smooth if you don't want it to be. You can add texture with the bristles of a brush, a scrunched-up piece of tin foil or other items to make this look like rough stone. Or smooth everything out with some air-dry clay slip, as I did. Once I was happy with the shape, I took my table knife and made some curved indents in the surface, for detail.

8. Leave to dry, moving from time to time to allow the whole piece to dry.

9. Sand, paint and seal.

DECORATION SUGGESTION

I gave the clay two full coats of a soft, sandy-coloured acrylic paint. I then speckled on darker and lighter tones, by adding a little water to the acrylic paint and tapping a loaded paintbrush with another brush to flick paint all over the piece. I finished with two coats of a matt acrylic varnish.

If you added texture, then dry brushing (p.22) works well to bring this out.

LITTLE BIRD COTTONBUD CADDY

There has to be something bird themed within this book – I am Red Rocking Bird, after all! I love sculpting 3D birds from air-dry clay, and this is a really simple design with a practical use. I've chosen to store cottonbuds in my little bird, but you could use it for matchsticks or toothpicks. You can adapt the shape into any other design, too!

WHAT YOU NEED

250g (8.8oz) air-dry clay
Pebble or ping-pong ball
Tin foil
2 pens
Tape
Acrylic paint
Paintbrushes and/or sponge
Sealant

Optional

Hot glue
Rolling pin

1. A pebble can give some extra weight inside the bird if you need it, but here I use a ping-pong ball to start the body of the bird. Rip a sheet of tin foil, scrunch it up and then 'un-scrunch' a little. Wrap the ball with the foil, adding more until you form a bird shape – imagine a round body and a round head joined together, with a slight point at the beak. The beauty of creating something like a bird is the dimensions can be as you wish. Use some hot glue if you need it.

2. Take half of the clay and pinch or roll it to about 8mm (⅜in) in thickness. Wrap the clay around the bird shape and smooth into the contours with your fingers. Keep adding flattened clay to the bird in small sections, blending and smoothing as you go, filling all the gaps, but not overlapping too much; try and blend the clay so that it is all one thickness around the bird shape.

3. Next, make the section where the cottonbuds will be stored, which will also be the tail of the bird. Take two pens and tape them neatly together at one end. Roll a piece of clay to 8mm (⅜in) thick and cut to 40mm (1½in) in width. Wrap it around the end of the pens and cut off the excess length. Use the score and slip method (p.20) to join the two edges. Remove the pens just for a moment to secure the inside, adding extra clay coils where necessary on the join, so you basically have a thick loop of clay.

4. With the pens back in the tail loop, bring it to the bird body – imagine the cottonbuds sitting in the holder and angle the tail upwards accordingly. Mark where this will go using a toothpick and score and slip as before. Then roll a thin coil and wrap this around the base of the tail, join and smooth.

5. Remove the pens once the tail is fully attached. Give the bird some more shape, giving definition to the wings and pinching the clay to form a slight beak. I also add a small 'V'-shaped notch at the tail.

6. Add some texture. I dabbed a scrunched-up piece of tin foil all over the clay surface. Place the bird upright on a flat surface, encouraging a flat area at the base so that it is stable. Prop up the tail using whatever items you have to hand and leave to dry.

7. I dabbed a mixture of brown, grey and white acrylic paints onto the bird with a brush and sponge, let it dry, and then sealed with a matt acrylic varnish.

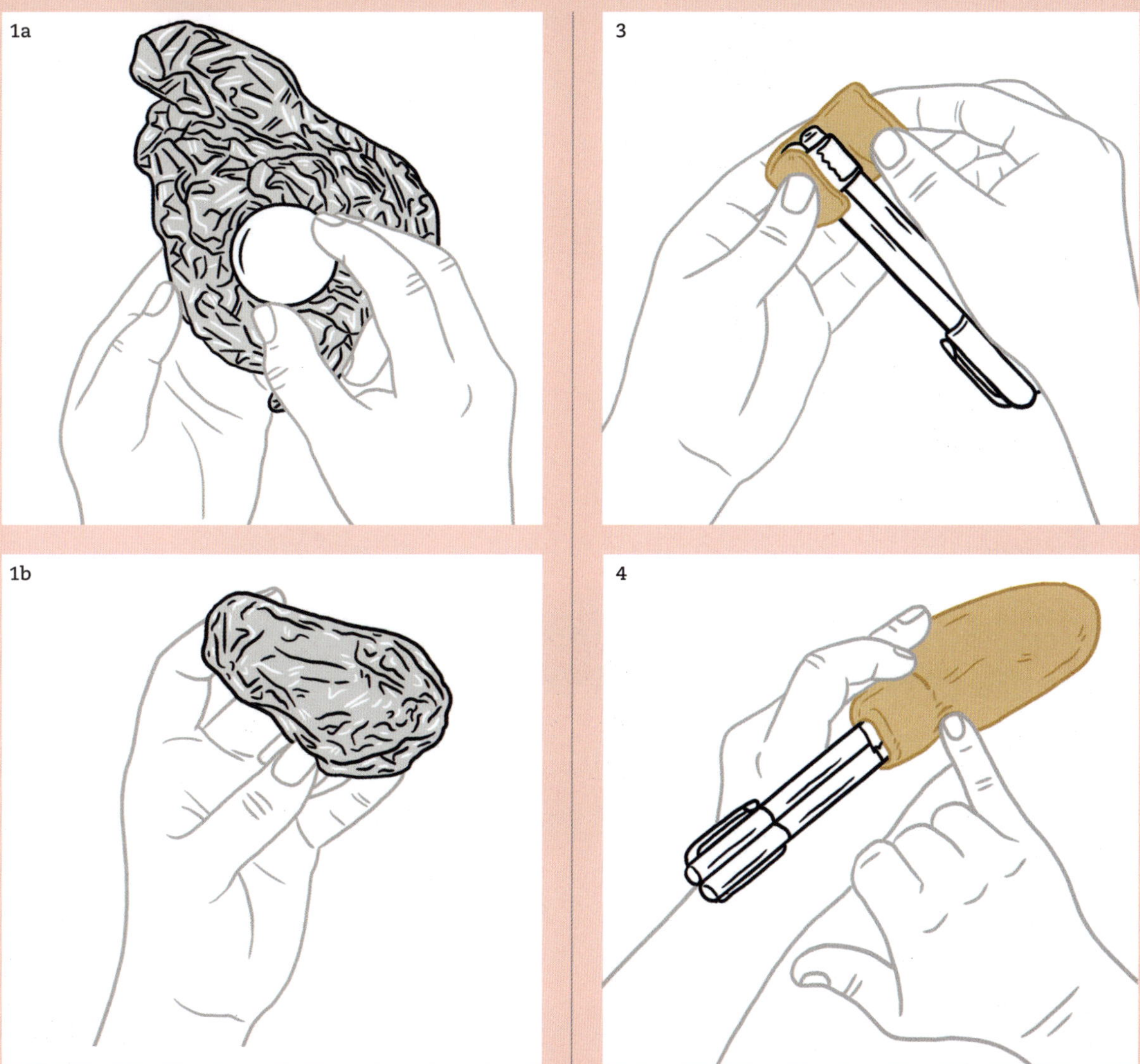
1a
3
1b
4

LIDDED POT

A timeless piece that would sit well in both modern and traditional homes – adjust the dimensions to make pots of various sizes. These would look lovely on a bedside table to hold trinkets, or by the front door as a place to store keys.

WHAT YOU NEED

1kg (2.2lb) air-dry clay
Rolling pin
Knife/scalpel
Ruler
A4 card
Toothpick
Round cookie cutter (or similar), 115mm (4½in) in diameter and one just smaller (see steps 2 and 4)
Paper
Pencil
Scissors
Paintbrush
Drinking straw or similar
Sandpaper
Paint
Sealant
100mm (4in) of thick twine/cord/leather strap

1. This pot uses the slab building technique, just like the Pen Pot on pp.102–7. Follow steps 1–9 from that tutorial, using the following quantities and dimensions, to make the bottom half of this pot.
   - 200g (7oz) clay, rolled to 10mm (⅜in) in thickness, cutting a 115mm (4½in) disc
   - 350g (12⅜oz) clay, rolled to 10mm (⅜in) in thickness, cut to the length of disc circumference and 45mm (1¾in) in height (there will be plenty of excess clay from both pieces to use later).

2. Once the base of the pot is complete, use another cookie cutter that fits just inside the rim of the pot to make sure it is still evenly circular. Set aside to start drying.

3. To make the pot lid, roll a 300g (10½oz) ball of clay to 10mm (⅜in) in thickness and cut another 115mm (4½in) disc. Smooth both sides. Whichever side is face down will be the top of the pot and we now work on the underside to make a lip for the pot lid.

4. With a ruler and sharp point, mark the centre-point of the clay disc. Then mark a rim around the inside of the disc with the cookie cutter that fits inside the pot base. If you do not have one, make a paper template that would fit just inside the pot and, using a toothpick, draw around this onto the disc of clay.

5. Roll some of the excess clay together and form a long coil approximately 10mm (⅜in) thick. Curl this around the inside of the mark you just made and cut to length where it meets.

6. Score the disc of clay just inside the circular mark, add some slip and press the coil on top. Use the score and slip technique (p.20) to secure this coil into place, using some slip on your finger and a brush or sponge to blend everything smooth. Make sure that the clay does not spread outwards of the circular mark, otherwise the lid will not fit on the pot once everything is dry.

7. Take a drinking straw or similar and cut a small round hole at the central point of the lid. (If the little piece of clay does not come out with the straw, leave it there and it will pop out once everything is dry.)

TIP

Make sure you are working on a surface that can be moved around easily so that you can access the clay by turning the board or cloth as you work.

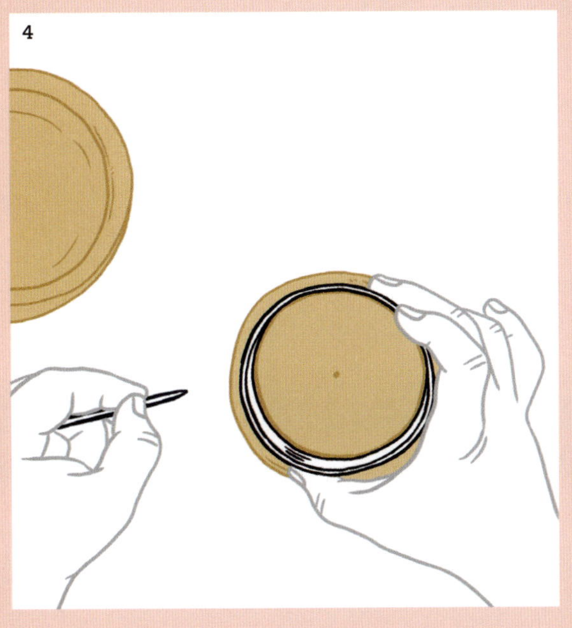
4

6a

6b

8. Set aside and leave to dry. Once the piece has started to firm up and dry, turn both pieces over. Any bumps on the underside can be smoothed out at this stage if need be. Dry fully, turning over from time to time. In the winter, where I live, I would leave this for a week to dry, as it is fairly thick in places.

9. Sand any imperfections with sandpaper, paint and seal.

10. Fold the twine/cord/leather strap in half and push the two tails through from the top of the lid. Hold the tails together and do a simple knot inside. This makes a little handle for the pot lid.

DECORATION SUGGESTION

The possibilities are endless with this simple shape, but I chose to apply a coat of white acrylic paint to the finished, dry pot. Once this was dry, I applied delicate 'streaks' or lines to the outside, in varying shades of green-grey. Hidden away inside the pot, like a little surprise, is a blue heart, painted freehand. I used gloss varnish over the whole piece for a shiny finish.

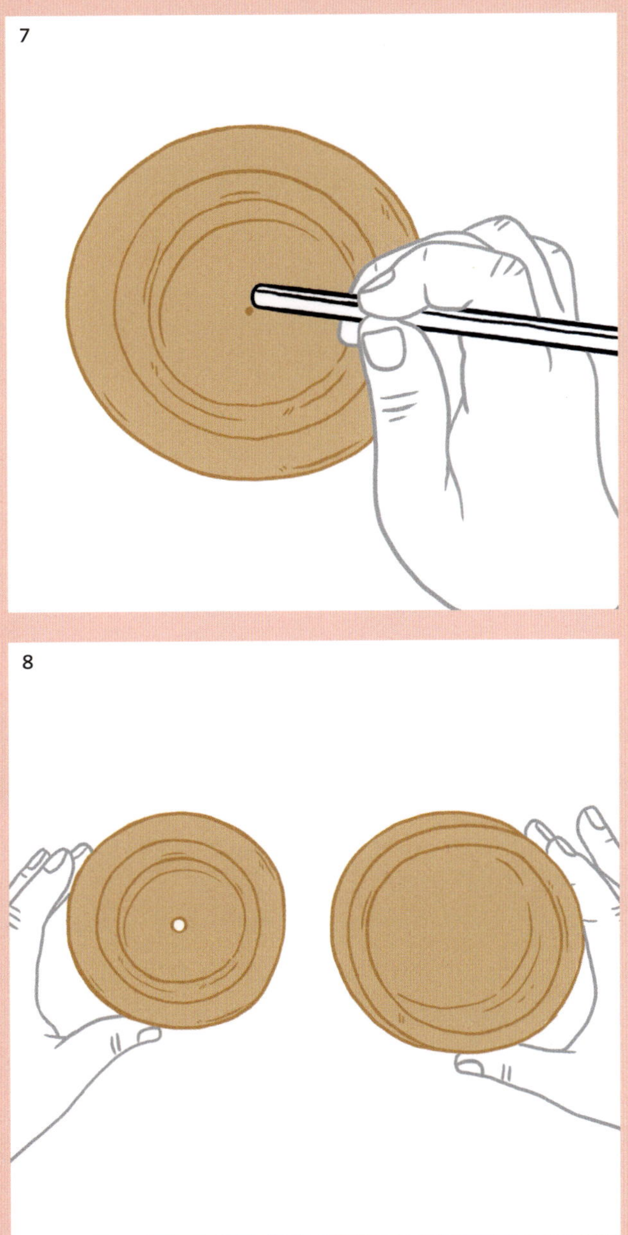
7
8

RIBBED PLANT POT

These pots, with their organic, tactile form, are much easier to make than you might think. I have experimented with different techniques to get the result I was after using the simplest method possible. Master this and you'll have a really 'arty' planter in your hands!

This project I left until last because, although it is fairly simple to create, it requires the confidence and ability to handle and support the clay in the final stages. Hopefully by now, if you have worked through the book, you do have this confidence.

WHAT YOU NEED

400g (14oz) air-dry clay
Small round jar or round yoghurt pot with the rim cut off
Paintbrushes
Paint
Sealant

Optional

Cardboard
Cling film

1. The equipment list is super simple, but you need to dedicate a good amount of time to this project. The body of the vase is created using the pinch pot technique. Start by shaping the whole 400g (14oz) of clay into a smooth oval shape; mine is 90mm (3½in) tall.

2. Hold the clay in your non-dominant hand and then press the thumb of the other hand into the centre of the clay.

3. Creating a paddle with your fingers, use a pinching motion to shape the clay as you rotate it. Create a slightly longer rather than just a rounded shape if you can, by pinching upwards towards the hole. If any cracks appear, smooth them out with some air-dry clay slip on your fingers. Keep repeating the pinching technique until the walls of clay are approximately 12mm (½in) thick. For example, my vase is now 90mm (3½in) tall and 80mm (3⅛in) wide, with a gap of approximately 65mm (2½in) on the inside. Your jar or pot should almost be able to fit inside now.

4. Find a paintbrush with a fairly thick handle (or the end of a marker pen would work, or a chopstick). Pick the clay up, placing three or four fingers inside to support it, then use the wrong end of the brush to draw an indent in the vase from rim to the base. Repeat all the way around the clay with approximately 20mm (¾in) between each indent.

5. Keeping hold of the clay in your non-dominant hand, put the brush down and pinch the clay between the indents with your thumb and forefinger, pinching all the way from the top of the vase to the base to form 'spines'. Repeat all around the vase.

6. It is likely that the clay will have started to crack a little in some areas. If so, take some air-dry clay slip on your fingers and smooth out any cracks. Or you can leave it more rustic if you prefer.

7. The inside of the vase can be shaped and smoothed at this point. I press and smooth my finger along the inside of the newly created 'spines', enlarging the space within the vase so that the jar or pot will fit inside with a little bit of extra room around it. This allows for shrinkage while the vase is drying.

TIP

If the shaping and sculpting is not quite coming together, then there is no harm in kneading the clay back up again with some slip on your hands (the clay could do with a bit of moisture by now). Maybe try making a smaller version first or make the walls even thicker at the start.

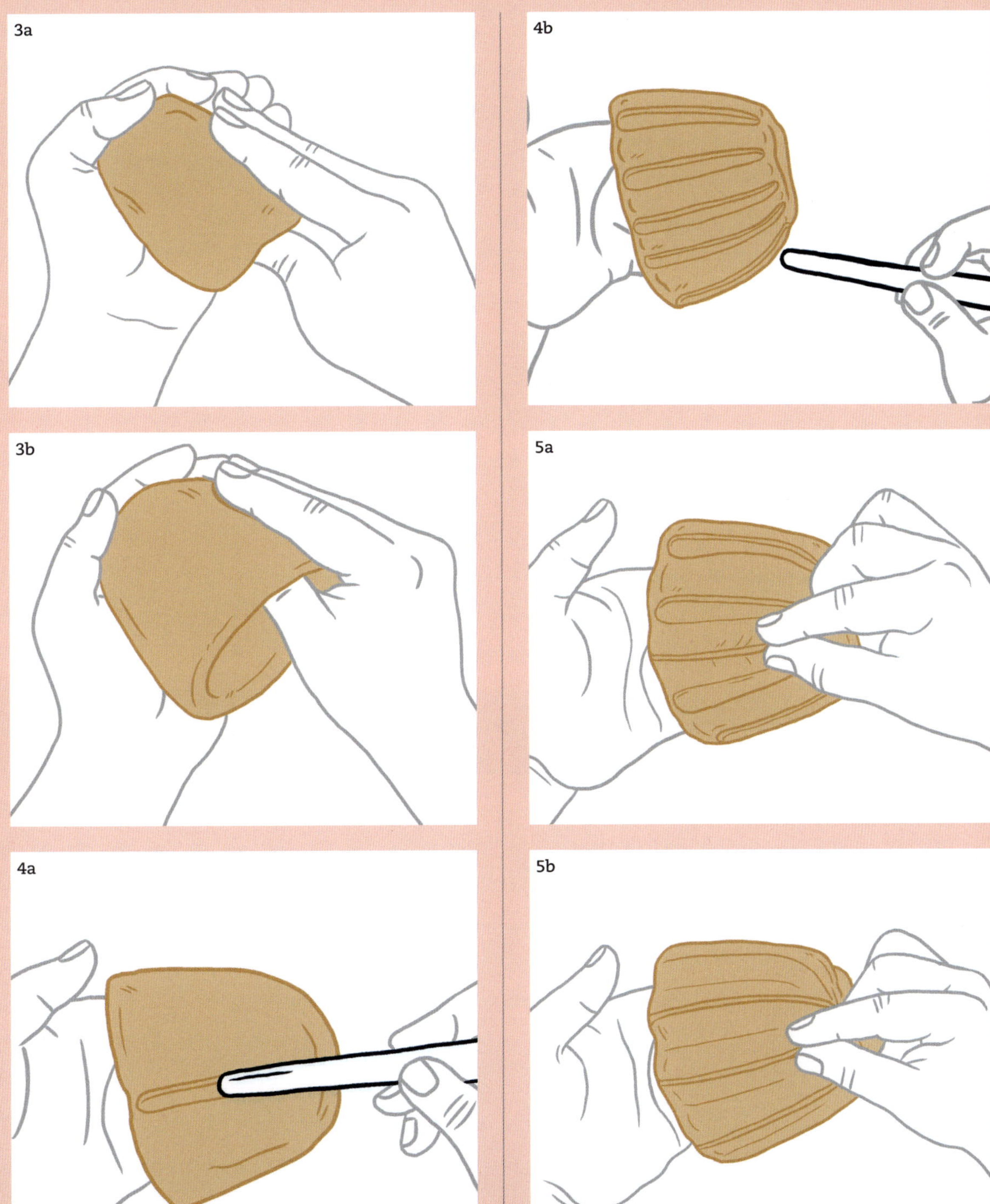
3a
4b
3b
5a
4a
5b

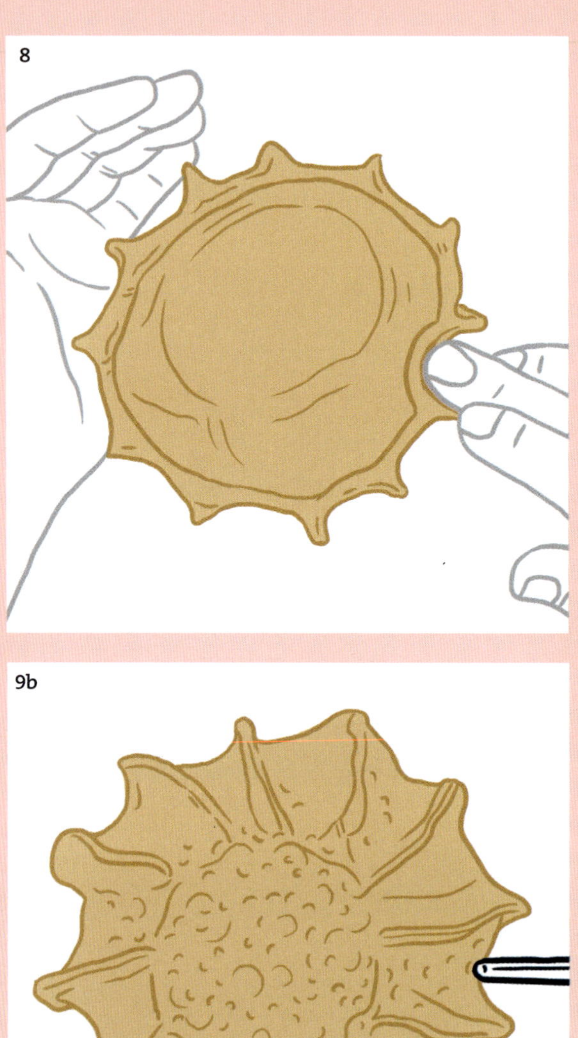
8
9b

DECORATION SUGGESTION

I painted the whole pot in a light grey acrylic paint, adding a little water to the paint to make it easier to apply to the textured surface. I then dabbed on some brown acrylic paint with a sponge, and dry brushed with white acrylic paint (p.22).

8. Shape the spines some more. The beauty of this project is its organic nature, so uneven spines are good – some longer and some a bit wavy. I encourage the rim of the vase to become wavy by creating 'dips' in the gaps between spines, and pinching the spines up and over. Make sure the clay doesn't get too thin – you should always have at least 2–3mm (⅛in) between your fingers. You can remove some clay between spines on the rim.

9. To add some texture, I used the other end of several paintbrushes and added light dimples into the surface of the clay. I also used the end of a drinking straw to add more variation of texture.

10. Once you are happy with the shape of your vase, it is time to support it to let it dry. I find it works best to take the jar or pot that is going to hold the water, wrap it in a couple of layers of card and then cling film and place inside the vase. Turn it all upside down and support from the inside with something that is taller than the pot, so that the rim is elevated. Flatten the base of the vase a little so that when it is turned over later, it will be stable. Leave to dry.

11. After about 24 hours, or when it has started to firm up, turn the vase over, remove the jar/pot, then leave to dry the correct way up until it is fully dry.

12. Paint and seal. I used two coats of matt acrylic varnish.

13. Now that you know how the shape comes together, have a play around with different volumes of clay – try and make either taller or wider pots depending on your preference.

TEMPLATES

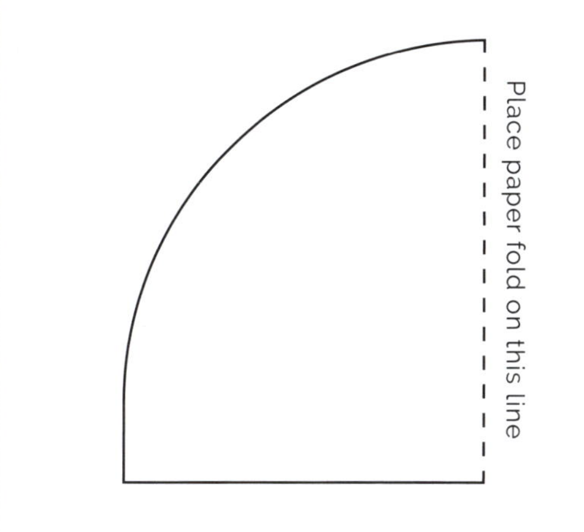

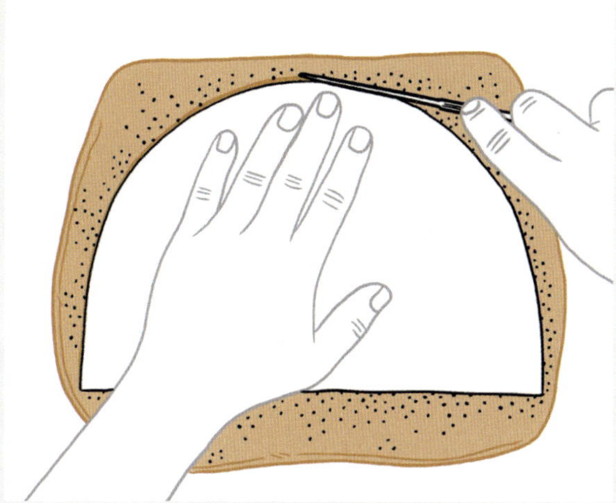

All templates are to scale. Use tracing paper and a pencil to copy the required template. If the template indicates a fold line, then fold your tracing paper in half and place the folded edge onto the line before tracing.

The traced shape can then be cut out – or glued to a piece of card first, and then cut out – ready to use in your project.

FLOWER 'FROG'

Page 33

LITTLE HOUSE PHOTO HOLDER

Page 36

BOTANICAL RING HOLDER

Page 44

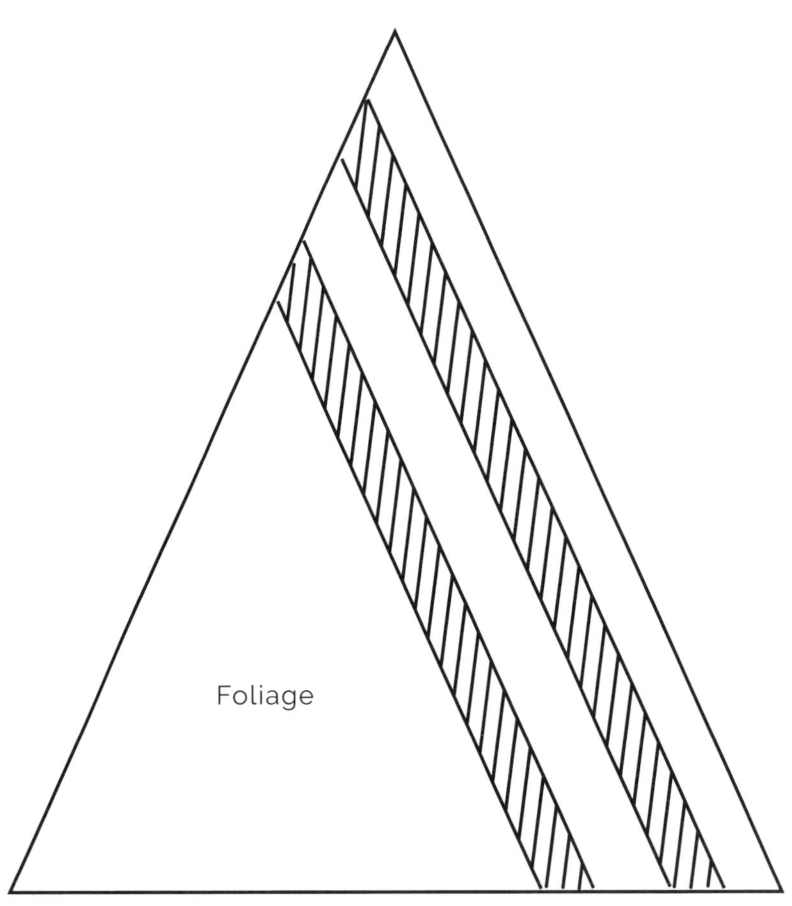

PRETTY MIRROR

Page 54

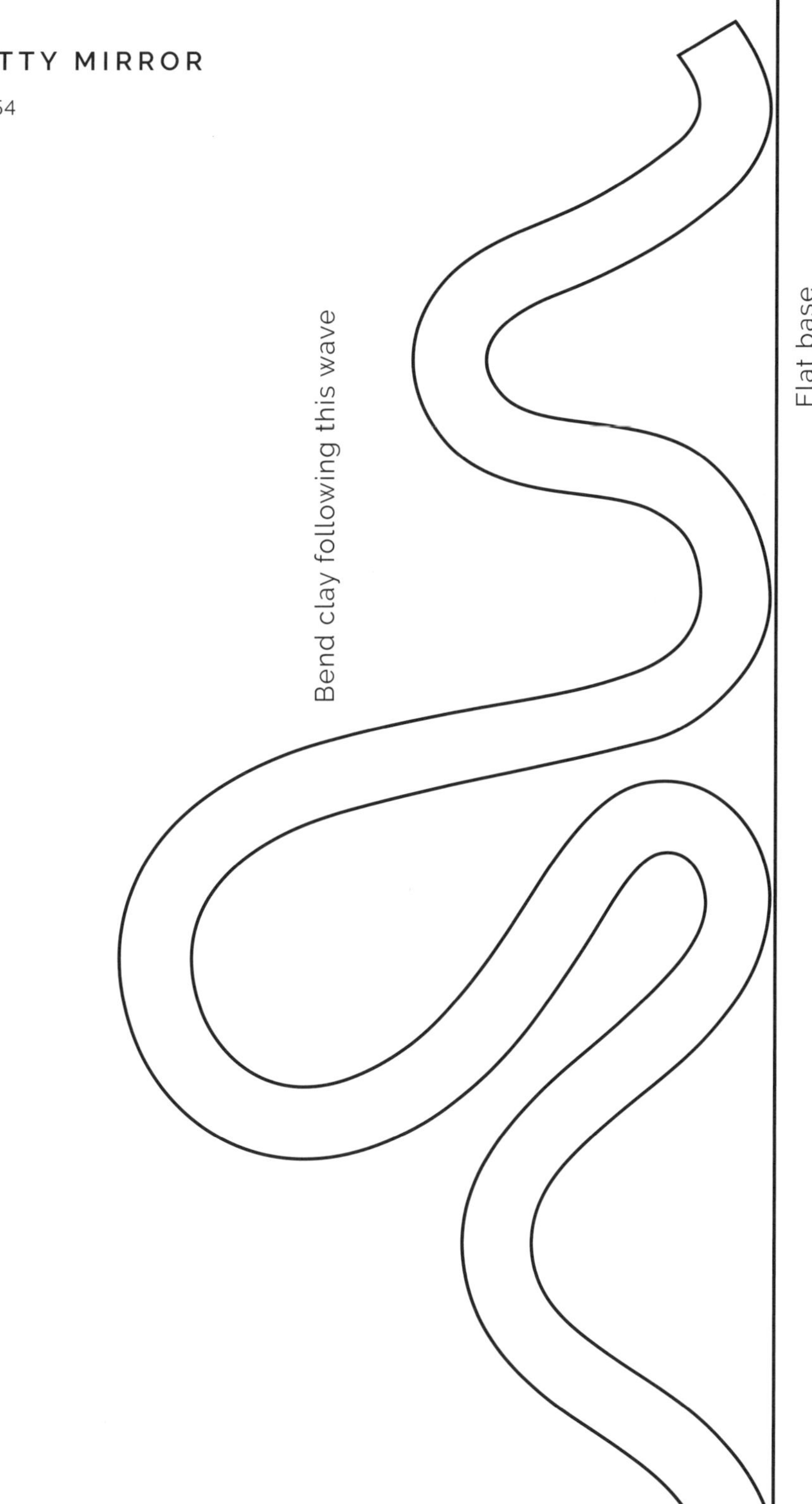

INCENSE STICK HOLDER

Page 65

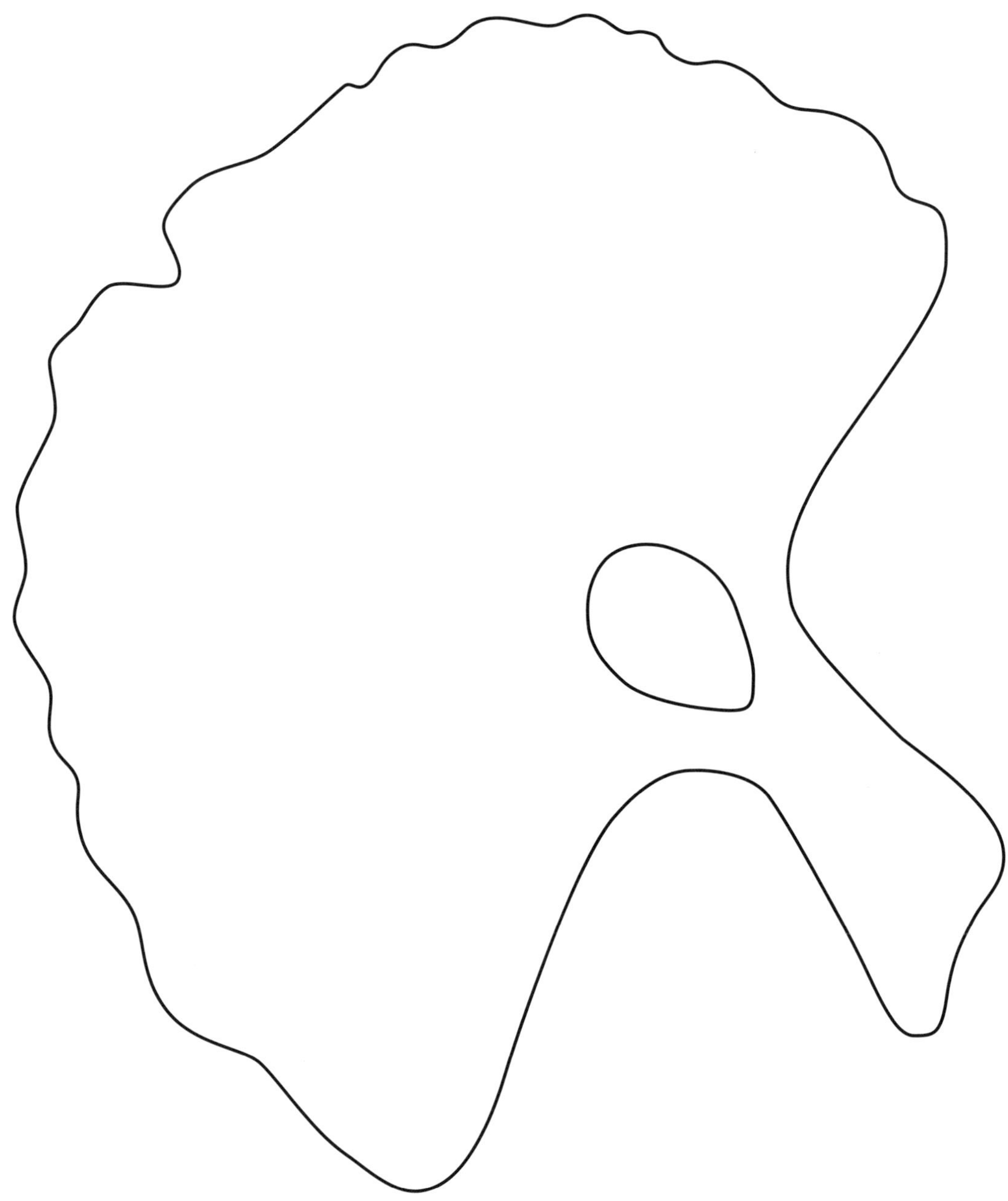

CANDLESTICK HOLDER

Page 91

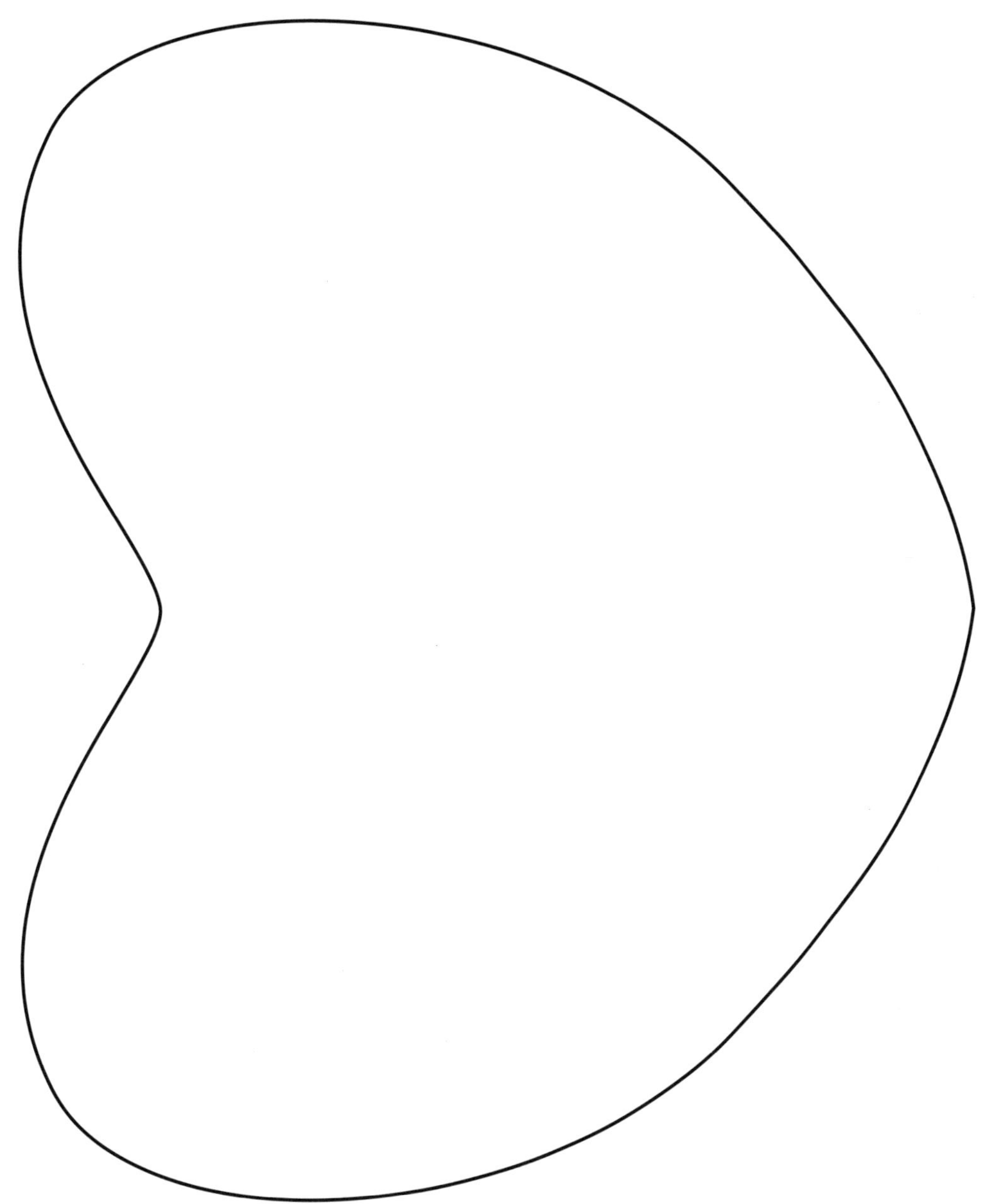

TEXTURED CLOCK

Page 73

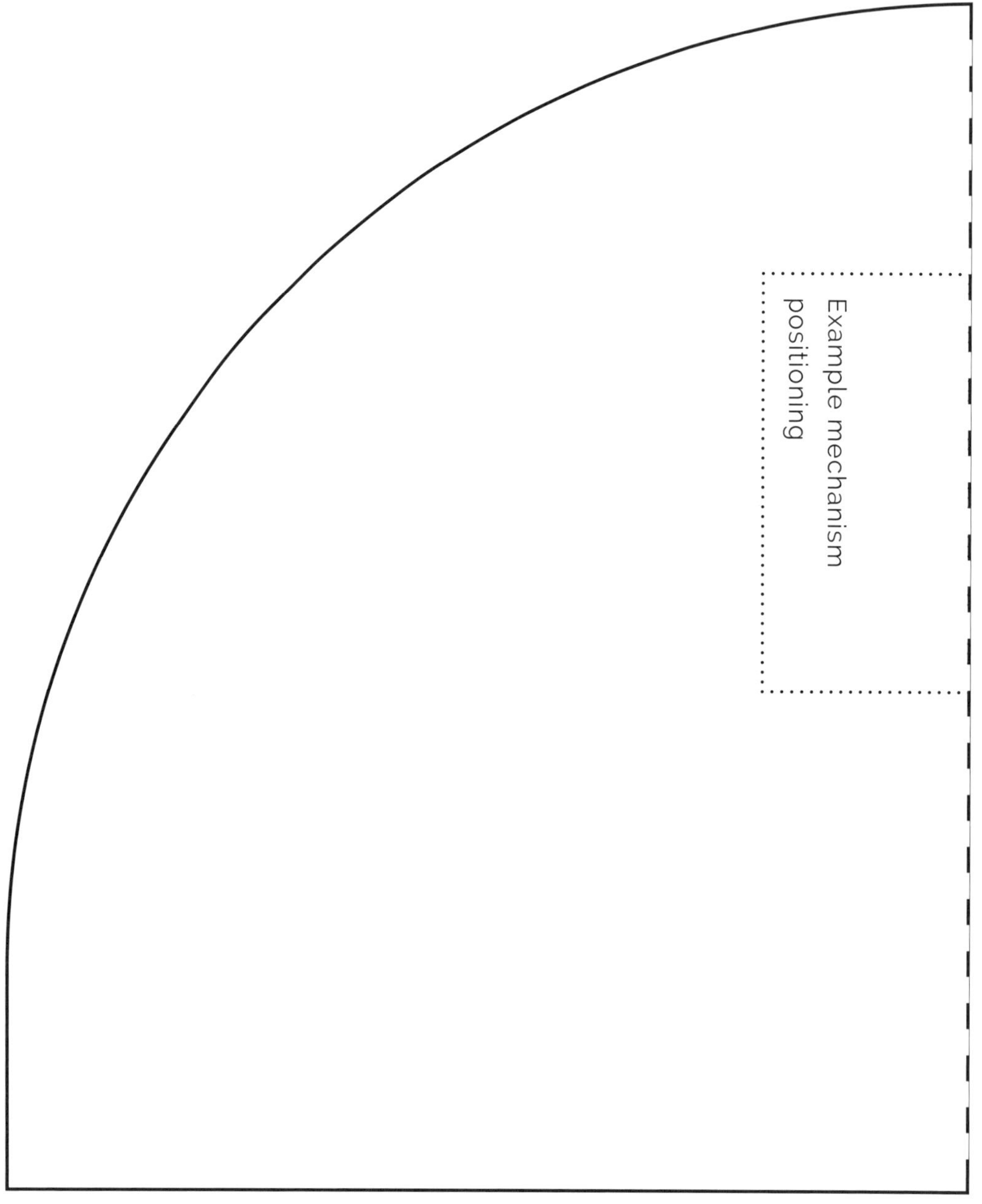

PEN POT (HEART)

Page 102

WALL-HANGING FLOWER POCKET

Page 86

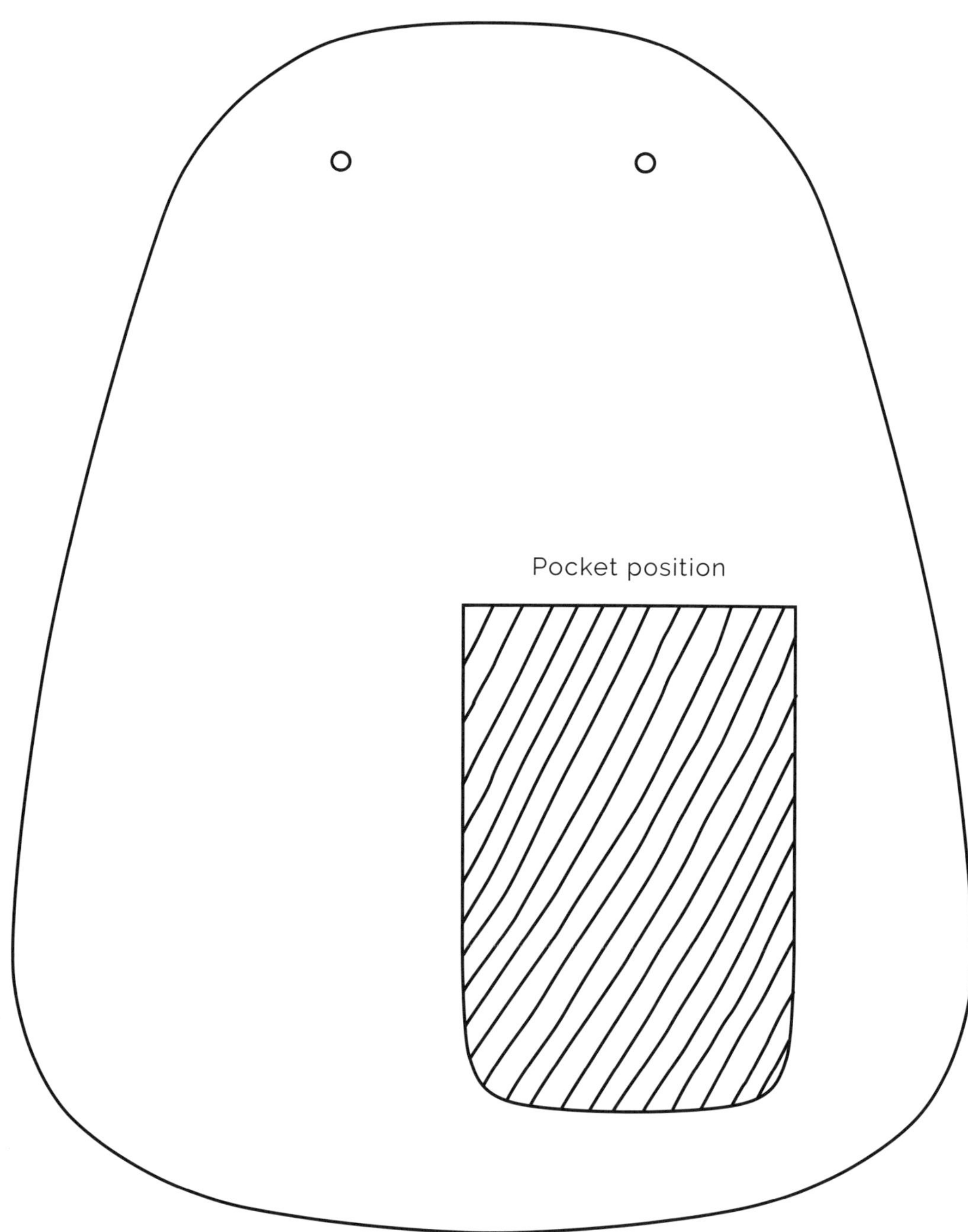

Pocket

BIOGRAPHY

From an early age, Sarah Reeves showed a deep interest in art and design. Her dream was to be an artist, and over the years she tried her hand at many creative projects, leaning towards three-dimensional design. Sarah gained a degree in Furniture and Product Design, where she learned all the fundamentals of design. Sarah has always had a passion for sculpting, and air-dry clay lets her do this at home with very few resources. This led Sarah to inspire others through creative tutorials on Youtube, where she is better known as Red Rocking Bird: 'Air-dry clay is amazing, therapeutic and so accessible to all, allowing everyone to immerse themselves in the creativity of clay.'

Sarah's Red Rocking Bird YouTube tutorials are known for being calm, positive and therapeutic and she has written this book with joy and passion, in the hope of inspiring you to be creative.

www.youtube.com/c/redrockingbird

ACKNOWLEDGEMENTS

Thank you to the team at Ilex/Octopus for believing in me and supporting the whole creation of this book.

I wrote this for my children, to reinforce the notion of following our dreams.

In memory of my amazing Mum, who lived life following her passions and dreams – my true inspiration.

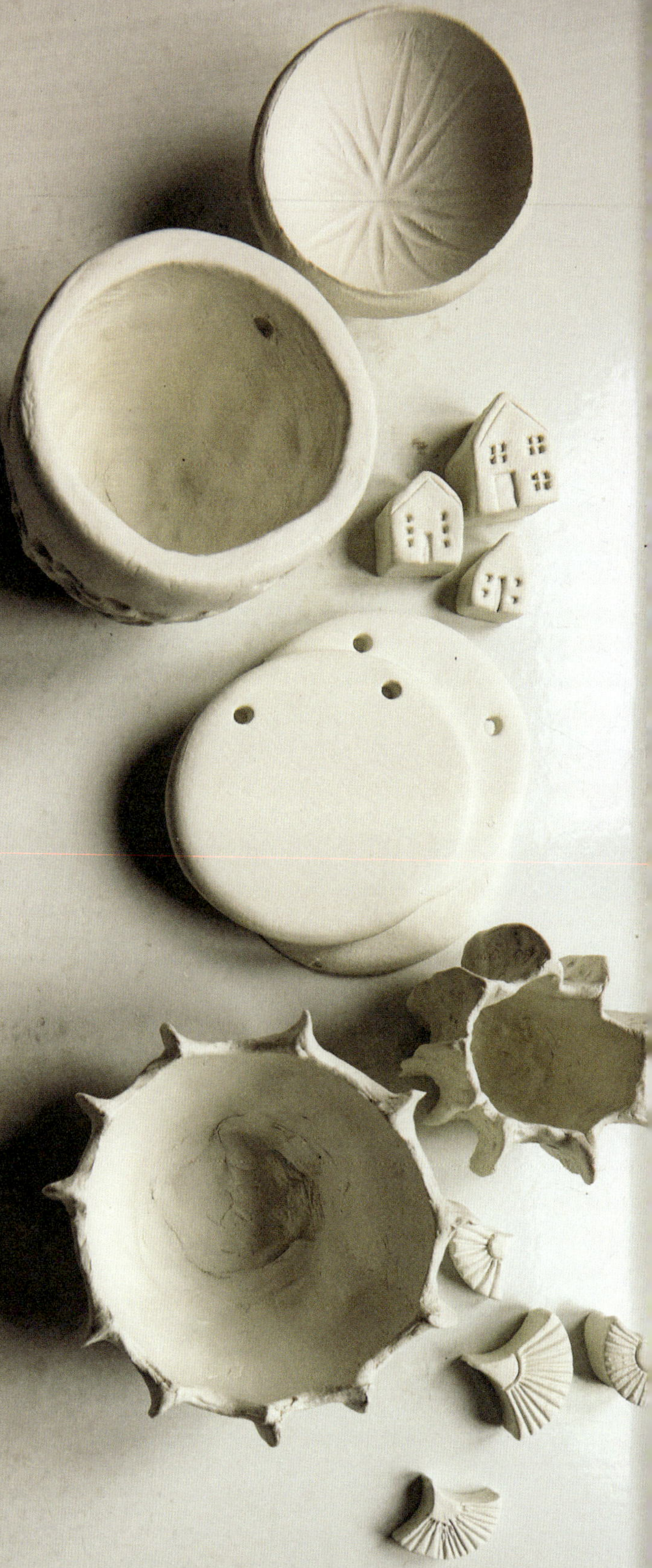

First published in Great Britain in 2025 by Ilex,
a division of Octopus Publishing Group Ltd
Carmelite House, 50 Victoria Embankment,
London, EC4Y 0DZ
www.octopusbooks.co.uk
www.octopusbooksusa.com

An Hachette UK Company
www.hachette.co.uk

The authorized representative in the EEA is Hachette Ireland, 8 Castlecourt Centre, Dublin 15, D15 XTP3, Ireland (email: info@hbgi.ie)

Distributed in the US by Hachette Book Group,
1290 Avenue of the Americas, 4th & 5th Floors,
New York, NY 10104

Distributed in Canada by Canadian Manda Group,
664 Annette Street, Toronto, Ontario M6S 2C8

ISBN 978-1-84091-917-2
eISBN 978-1-84091-918-9

A CIP catalogue record for this book is available from the British Library

Printed and bound in China

10 9 8 7 6 5 4 3 2 1

Publisher: Alison Starling
Assistant Editor: Ellen Sleath
Managing Editor: Rachel Silverlight
Project Editor: Faye Robson
Art Director: Ben Gardiner
Photography: Kim Lightbody
Prop Stylist: Rachel Vere
Illustrations: Caitlin Keegan
Design: Jane Lanaway
Production Manager: Lisa Pinnell